READINGS ON

J.R.R. TOLKIEN

THE GREENHAVEN PRESS
Literary Companion
TO BRITISH AUTHORS

J.R.R. TOLKIEN

Katie de Koster, *Book Editor*

David L. Bender, *Publisher*
Bruno Leone, *Executive Editor*
Bonnie Szumski, *Series Editor*

Greenhaven Press, Inc., San Diego, CA

Every effort has been made to trace the owners of copyrighted material. The articles in this volume may have been edited for content, length, and/or reading level. The titles have been changed to enhance the editorial purpose. Those interested in locating the original source will find the complete citation on the first page of each article.

Library of Congress Cataloging-in-Publication Data

Readings on J.R.R. Tolkien / Katie de Koster, book editor.
        p.   cm. — (The Greenhaven Press literary companion to British authors)
    Includes bibliographical references and index.
    ISBN 0-7377-0245-1 (lib. bdg. : alk. paper). —
ISBN 0-7377-0244-3 (pbk. : alk. paper)
    1. Tolkien, J.R.R. (John Ronald Reuel), 1892–1973—
Criticism and interpretation. 2. Tolkien, J.R.R. (John Ronald Reuel), 1892–1973. Lord of the rings. 3. Tolkien, J.R.R. (John Ronald Reuel), 1892–1973. Hobbit. 4. Fantasy fiction, English—History and criticism. 5. Middle Earth (Imaginary place) I. De Koster, Katie, 1948–   . II. Series
PR6039.032Z798   2000
828'.91209—dc21
                                                                    99-34336
                                                                         CIP

Copyright © 2000 by Greenhaven Press, Inc.
PO Box 289009
San Diego, CA 92198-9009
Printed in the U.S.A.

I write things that might be classified as fairy-stories not because I wish to address children . . . but because I wish to write this kind of story and no other.

—J.R.R. Tolkien

CONTENTS

FOREWORD

*"'Tis the good reader that
makes the good book."*

Ralph Waldo Emerson

The story's bare facts are simple: The captain, an old and scarred seafarer, walks with a peg leg made of whale ivory. He relentlessly drives his crew to hunt the world's oceans for the great white whale that crippled him. After a long search, the ship encounters the whale and a fierce battle ensues. Finally the captain drives his harpoon into the whale, but the harpoon line catches the captain about the neck and drags him to his death.

A simple story, a straightforward plot—yet, since the 1851 publication of Herman Melville's *Moby-Dick*, readers and critics have found many meanings in the struggle between Captain Ahab and the whale. To some, the novel is a cautionary tale that depicts how Ahab's obsession with revenge leads to his insanity and death. Others believe that the whale represents the unknowable secrets of the universe and that Ahab is a tragic hero who dares to challenge fate by attempting to discover this knowledge. Perhaps Melville intended Ahab as a criticism of Americans' tendency to become involved in well-intentioned but irrational causes. Or did Melville model Ahab after himself, letting his fictional character express his anger at what he perceived as a cruel and distant god?

Although literary critics disagree over the meaning of *Moby-Dick*, readers do not need to choose one particular interpretation in order to gain an understanding of Melville's

9

novel. Instead, by examining various analyses, they can gain numerous insights into the issues that lie under the surface of the basic plot. Studying the writings of literary critics can also aid readers in making their own assessments of *Moby-Dick* and other literary works and in developing analytical thinking skills.

The Greenhaven Literary Companion Series was created with these goals in mind. Designed for young adults, this unique anthology series provides an engaging and comprehensive introduction to literary analysis and criticism. The essays included in the Literary Companion Series are chosen for their accessibility to a young adult audience and are expertly edited in consideration of both the reading and comprehension levels of this audience. In addition, each essay is introduced by a concise summation that presents the contributing writer's main themes and insights. Every anthology in the Literary Companion Series contains a varied selection of critical essays that cover a wide time span and express diverse views. Wherever possible, primary sources are represented through excerpts from authors' notebooks, letters, and journals and through contemporary criticism.

Each title in the Literary Companion Series pays careful consideration to the historical context of the particular author or literary work. In-depth biographies and detailed chronologies reveal important aspects of authors' lives and emphasize the historical events and social milieu that influenced their writings. To facilitate further research, every anthology includes primary and secondary source bibliographies of articles and/or books selected for their suitability for young adults. These engaging features make the Greenhaven Literary Companion series ideal for introducing students to literary analysis in the classroom or as a library resource for young adults researching the world's great authors and literature.

Exceptional in its focus on young adults, the Greenhaven Literary Companion Series strives to present literary criticism in a compelling and accessible format. Every title in the series is intended to spark readers' interest in leading American and world authors, to help them broaden their understanding of literature, and to encourage them to formulate their own analyses of the literary works that they read. It is the editors' hope that young adult readers will find these anthologies to be true companions in their study of literature.

INTRODUCTION

Readers generally do not need to be encouraged to enjoy reading J.R.R. Tolkien's most famous works, *The Hobbit* and *The Lord of the Rings*. They are drawn into the pages, engaged by the stories, reluctant to put the books down, and sad when they reach the end.

Like any good mythology—which is what Tolkien was consciously creating—the books can be enjoyed on many levels. They resonate differently and offer different views and shades of meanings depending on what the reader brings to the experience. But beyond understanding the tale of the quest, for example, or the religious significance of The One, or the nature of heroism, there is another asset of great value in Tolkien's work that can be mined painlessly: language.

Not "languages," such as Quenya, the High-elven tongue, but the mastery of language. Tolkien was a prose poet who loved words, loved how words work together, and who had a master's understanding of the underpinnings of how we communicate with words. His command of the language is such that the reader will be tempted to simply dive in and allow the rush of words to flow and surge. But once in a while, stand back and look at what Tolkien has wrought. See how he puts the words together. Observe the precise use of grammar and punctuation as well as nouns and verbs. Appreciate the shadings and nuances as he creates an entire mythology with words that seem to come alive. There has been no one else like him, and may never be again.

J.R.R. Tolkien: Maker of Worlds

The birth of John Ronald Reuel Tolkien in Bloemfontein, South Africa, was quite an event. With his eyes of English blue and a bit of very fair hair topping an unusually high brow, he was such a curiosity that his parents' houseboy, Isaak, "borrowed" him for a while to take him into his village and show him off. Since Isaak's excursion with the baby was unauthorized, it caused quite a bit of turmoil. Fortunately for Isaak, the Tolkiens—especially young Ronald's mother—were understanding. In gratitude for their tolerance, Isaak named his own son Isaak Mister Tolkien Victor.

Mabel and Arthur Tolkien

Both of Ronald's parents were from Birmingham, England, where financial conditions were difficult at the end of the nineteenth century. Arthur Reuel Tolkien's family had once manufactured pianos, but they had lost the firm and Arthur's father had gone bankrupt. Mabel Suffield's father had owned a drapery business, but he too had suffered bankruptcy. Thus when Arthur proposed to Mabel shortly after her eighteenth birthday, her father objected to their betrothal both on grounds of her youth (Arthur was thirteen years older than she was) and because Arthur's position in the Birmingham branch of Lloyd's Bank did not pay well enough to support a family. The couple wrote letters to each other in secret—Mabel's sister Jane acted as go-between, making the exchange with Arthur on a train platform on her way home from school—while waiting for her to reach the age of twenty-one, when her father would no longer be able to forbid her to marry.

Although John Suffield, Mabel's father, would not allow them to announce a formal betrothal, Mabel had accepted Arthur's proposal. With this new incentive to succeed, he sought a banking position with better prospects, and soon accepted a position with the Bank of Africa. By the end of 1890 he was manager of the branch in Bloemfontein, the capital of the Orange Free State, now part of South Africa. It provided not only an adequate income but also a home, Bank House on Maitland Street, with servants. Mabel turned twenty-one in January 1891 and shortly afterward sailed for South Africa to marry Arthur. They were married in Cape Town on April 16.

After a short honeymoon, the newlyweds made the grueling seven-hundred-mile rail journey to their new home in Bloemfontein. The town was an oasis of civilization in the veldt, where wolves and jackals roamed just a few hundred yards from the houses. The extremes of temperature in summer and winter were far from what they were used to, and even the winters were dry and dusty. When Mabel wrote home, she described the place as "'Owlin' Wilderness! Horrid Waste!" But Arthur was happy there, if not as healthy as she would have liked, so she tried to settle in, realizing unhappily that they would not be eligible for "home leave"—a chance to visit England—for another three years.

Arthur was often busy—when not at the bank, he was often studying Dutch, the language of business and government in colonial South Africa, or cultivating useful acquaintances to help his bank succeed in its rivalry with the native National Bank. Mabel became pregnant almost immediately, and her first son was born on January 3, 1892. They named him John, for Mabel's father; Reuel, after Arthur's middle name; and Ronald, which was what his family came to call him. John Ronald Reuel Tolkien was christened in Bloemfontein's Anglican cathedral on January 31.

FROM AFRICA BACK TO ENGLAND

Toddlers in Bloemfontein were exposed to a variety of rather exotic dangers. Tolkien biographer Humphrey Carpenter reports that a neighbor's pet monkeys climbed over the wall and chewed up young Tolkien's pinafores, and that the woodshed was a favorite lurking spot for snakes. Carpenter highlights one incident in which, just as he was learning to walk, young Ronald came upon a tarantula in the garden. It bit him and he ran screaming until his nurse caught him and treated the wound. In later years, the author remembered the terror he felt running through the grass on that hot day. Although he said he did not remember the tarantula itself, Tolkien's writings include more than one monstrous spider with a poisonous bite.

By that winter, Mabel was making no secret of her intense

dislike of the living conditions in Bloemfontein; she hated the climate, the tedious social life, and especially the fact that Arthur seemed so happy there, that she feared he would never agree to return to England. She began making plans for their home leave, but had to postpone them when she found herself pregnant again. Hilary Arthur Reuel, Ronald's brother, was born on February 17, 1894.

While Hilary seemed to thrive in South Africa, Ronald did not; the summer heat that year exacerbated the fever of teething, and Mabel became determined to take him to a cooler place for his health. In November she took the two boys to the coast near Cape Town for a vacation. Once they were back in Bloemfontein, with the boys now healthy enough for the long voyage, she began planning their home leave.

Although he wanted to accompany his young family, Arthur would not be able to go with them immediately, for business and financial reasons—he was needed in important railway negotiations, and during his home leave time he would receive only half pay. Mabel and the boys, with a nurse Arthur engaged for the journey, sailed for England in April 1895. Ronald later remembered watching Arthur paint his name on the lid of a trunk they would take with them; it was his only clear memory of his father.

Mabel and her sons stayed with her parents in Birmingham. She was glad to see that Ronald's health improved over the spring and summer, but unhappy that business further delayed Arthur in South Africa. In November he contracted rheumatic fever, which damages the heart, and did not want to attempt the long journey or face the English winter until he was well. By January, when he was still ill, Mabel decided to return to South Africa to care for him. Arrangements for the return trip had been completed when word arrived that Arthur had suffered a severe hemorrhage and died on February 15, 1896, just two days before Hilary's second birthday. He was buried in Bloemfontein.

Grief and guilt had to be put aside as Mabel, called Mab, turned to the problem of providing for her sons. She found a cheap semidetached row house in the village of Sarehole, in the countryside just outside Birmingham, a wonderful place for boys to play and explore. She also began to prepare Ronald for the entrance exams at his father's old school, King Edward VI School in Birmingham, which had an excellent reputation. Mabel was a linguist and taught her son Latin and German (both of which he enjoyed), as well as French (which for some reason did not appeal to him). Mab also taught him drawing and painting and supplied him with plenty of books to read. (He was especially taken with a story in the *Red Fairy Book* by Andrew Lang, about the dragon Fafnir; he later remembered, "I desired dragons with a profound desire.") She taught both boys botany, with disparate results: Ronald became especially good at drawing plants, while Hilary grew up to be a farmer.

ROMAN CATHOLICISM

Mab earned little income after her husband died, but both the Suffields and Tolkiens offered some financial help. However, in 1900, Mab converted to Roman Catholicism, which horrified and outraged both her own family and her in-laws. The Suffields withdrew their financial support and she and the boys became somewhat estranged from her family. Arthur's side of the family also objected strongly, although one of Ronald's uncles did agree to supply the twelve pounds per year needed for him to attend King Edward VI School when he passed the entrance examination on his second try, in 1900.

Mab knew that if Ronald was going to attend university, he would need to do well enough in school to win a scholarship. King Edward School was the best in Birmingham, but it was four miles from their home in Sarehole. Ronald walked to and from school for a few weeks, but with the onset of winter Mab decided to move the family closer to the school. After four happy years in their little cottage, they moved into town, to a house near King's Heath station that was right next to the railroad tracks. The trains were noisy and made the neighborhood less desirable, but Ronald was fascinated by the Welsh names painted on the rail cars that carried coal to the nearby coalyard. Captivated by such words as *Penrhiw-ceiber*, he added a lifelong love of the Welsh language to his other linguistic enthusiasms.

Although Mab had chosen the King's Heath house in part because of its proximity to St. Dunstan's Catholic Church, she soon decided she did not care for that church and began visiting others in the area. Thus she discovered the Birmingham Oratory, a large church with a community of priests and its own school, St. Philip's, which set lower fees than King Edward's and would provide her sons with a Roman Catholic education. In early 1902, they moved to Edgbaston, where the

Oratory was located, and the boys were enrolled in St. Philip's. The parish priest, Father Francis Xavier Morgan, soon became a good friend of the family, offering affection and a fatherly presence in the boys' lives that had been missing since they had become estranged from their relatives.

Ronald and Hilary were students of very different natures. Hilary was an indifferent student, whereas Ronald outpaced his new classmates so quickly that Mab soon realized he would need to return to King Edward's to get a good education. Mab withdrew them both from St. Philip's and resumed schooling them at home. Ronald won a Foundation Scholarship to King Edward's, returning there in the fall of 1903, while Hilary continued to study at home with their mother.

A Passion for Languages

At King Edward's, Ronald began learning Greek; he later noted, "The fluidity of Greek, punctuated by its hardness, and with its surface glitter captivated me. But part of the attraction was antiquity and alien remoteness (from me): it did not touch home." He found that he disliked Shakespeare, but—guided by medievalist George Brewerton, an enthusiastic teacher who had the students read the *Canterbury Tales*—he found another language to love. Middle English did not have the glitter of Greek or the euphony of Welsh; instead, Tolkien became interested in the language because it was the historical antecedent to his own tongue. He decided to investigate the history of languages.

As 1904 began, though, the entire household was ill. The boys had measles, followed by whooping cough; Hilary also had pneumonia. Although all of these diseases can be prevented or treated today, a century ago there were no powerful antibiotics. The strain of nursing the boys took its toll on their mother; by April 1904 Mabel was taken to the hospital, where she was diagnosed as diabetic.

This was long before insulin was developed as a treatment for diabetes. The illness was so serious that the family's house was closed, the furniture put into storage, and the boys sent to different Suffield relatives. Mab remained in the hospital until June, when she was released with the understanding that she would require a long convalescence.

Father Francis found a place for the three Tolkiens to live together, sharing a cottage with a postman and his wife on the grounds of a country retreat for the Oratory clergy, in Rednal. The setting was much like the happy home they had shared in Sarehole: The Tills, with whom they shared the cottage, saw they were well fed, and the boys delighted in an idyllic existence for the rest of the summer.

When fall arrived, it was time for Ronald to return to King Edward's, but Mab was reluctant to return to their drab existence in Birmingham. Instead, Ronald walked a mile each way to the station and took the train into town. As the days shortened, he would arrive home in the dark, often met by Hilary with a lantern.

The boys did not realize their mother's condition was deteriorating until she suddenly collapsed in early November. Sinking into a diabetic coma, she died on November 14, 1904. Ronald was twelve.

Their mother's death obviously changed the boys' physical circumstances, but it also had several less tangible effects on Ronald. She had introduced him to languages; her death strengthened his love of words, as it honored and maintained a connection with her. Their happiest times had been in rural settings, which became emotionally charged for Ronald after his mother's death. Mab's death also changed him emotionally. He had been a cheerful boy, and after she died he maintained a cheerful face in company. But in private, he developed a profound pessimism; her sudden death, after the idyllic summer, gave him a sense not only of loss, but of impermanence. It made him feel, as his biographer Humphrey Carpenter puts it, "Nothing was safe. Nothing would last. No battle would be won forever."

LIFE AS AN ORPHAN

Mabel had made Father Francis the boys' guardian. At first he did not want the boys to go to live with relatives since some of their kin wanted to contest the terms of her will and send the boys to a Protestant boarding school. Finally, though, Father Francis discovered that one of the boys' aunts, Beatrice Suffield, had a spare bedroom to offer and no strong religious views. Father Francis moved them into her home in Edgbaston.

Unfortunately, Aunt Beatrice, recently widowed herself, had little affection or understanding to offer the boys. The boys made the Oratory their unofficial home, spending as much time there as possible. Hilary was now a student at King Edward's too, so they walked to school together after helping at morning mass. Father Francis supplemented the small funds left by their mother with family money of his own, so they did not lack for material necessities.

Ronald's fellow student Christopher Wiseman became his inseparable companion and friendly rival for first place in their class. They shared interests in Latin and Greek, in rugby, and in discussing everything. They moved up from Fifth Class to First (senior) Class together. It was in First Class that the headmaster, Robert Cary Gilson, introduced them to the study not just of language, but of linguistics. Encouraged by Gilson, Ronald began to study the general principles of language, while the loan of an Anglo-Saxon primer from his Chaucer master, Brewerton, led him not only to the roots of his own language but to the great Old English poem *Beowulf.* Moving forward in time to Middle English, he read the medieval poem-story *Sir Gawain and the Green Knight* and *The Pearl,* an allegorical poem said to have been written by *Sir Gawain*'s author. Reading these classics in their original languages fired his passion; he was soon studying Old Norse so he could read the original tale of Fafnir the dragon, which he had enjoyed years ago in Andrew Lang's retelling of the tale. On his own, he scoured the shelves of the local bookshop, eventually coming across studies of philology (the study of literature and related disciplines) in German that helped him understand the structure of languages.

And then the young author took the next logical step: He began making up languages of his own. At first he used existing languages, such as Welsh and Spanish (a favorite of Father Francis's), as his starting point. After buying a copy of Joseph Wright's *Primer of the Gothic Language,* he discovered that only a few fragments of the written language survived, and he decided to fill in the gaps. He often discussed his efforts with his friend Christopher Wiseman, who was himself involved in studying the Egyptian language and hieroglyphics.

EDITH BRATT

In the meantime, when Ronald was fifteen, Father Francis realized the brothers were unhappy at their aunt's and moved them into a boardinghouse run by a Mrs. Faulkner. Another lodger there was also an orphan, nineteen-year-old Edith Bratt. She was an attractive girl with a gift for music. However, while Mrs. Faulkner encouraged Edith to play the piano at her evening musical soirees, she had no patience for practice arpeggios and scales. Edith spent more of her time in her room, at her sewing machine.

Ronald was sixteen and had been reared almost exclusively in the company of males. Understandably shy, he found it difficult to hold a conversation with a girl, but living in the same boardinghouse quickly broke down his reserve. The two became allies against the landlady (who never seemed to provide enough food to satisfy the growing adolescents). By the summer of 1909, they were in love.

Ronald was supposed to be studying diligently in order to win a scholarship to Oxford University, but he was pursuing other interests instead: inventing languages, thinking about Edith and seeing her away from the boardinghouse when he could, and joining the senior debating society at school. An indistinct speaker whose voice still occasionally squeaked, he had not done much public speaking, but he found joy in forming arguments and confounding his opponents by delivering them not in the Latin they expected, but in Gothic, Greek, or Anglo-Saxon.

Ronald and Edith thought they had been discreet about their relationship, but word of it eventually reached Father Francis, who was appalled. He berated Ronald, both for neglecting the studies that were his only hope for a good education and for carrying on a secret relationship with a girl who lived in the same house. He moved the boys out of the boardinghouse, then became infuriated when the couple began meeting again (although he had not expressly forbidden them to see each other). Eventually Edith decided to move to Cheltenham to live with a family who had befriended her. Father Francis ordered Ronald not to see or write Edith again until he was twenty-one and out of his guardianship, except for one last meeting on the day of her departure to say goodbye. Before she left, though, the two exchanged brief words during a few accidental meetings—the boys still lived nearby—and Father Francis found out. He called Ronald evil and foolish, and threatened to block his entrance to the university. Edith and Ronald would have to wait three years to see each other again, with no communication between them in the meantime.

Father Francis did not intend to be cruel; he felt his orders were in the best interests of his charge and improved his chances for a good education. But he was, perhaps, foolish; he certainly did not understand Ronald well enough to foresee the effect of his decision. For the next three years, Ronald would romanticize his relationship with Edith, focusing his plans and hopes on her. At the same time, since he was promised to her, he avoided other female company, spending all his time with male friends. In later years, he would compartmentalize his relationship with his wife and family from his camaraderie with his fellow scholars.

OXFORD

Ronald first took the scholarship exams for Oxford during the height of the blowup over Edith, and he failed to win an award. He could try again the following year, but in the meantime he needed to work harder at his studies at King Edward's. With Edith gone, relations with Father Francis strained, and depression setting in, he turned all his attention to school. In 1911 he and Christopher Wiseman, along with R.Q. Gilson (son of the headmaster of King Edward's) and a few other boys, founded the Tea Club. They began by having tea in the library—a forbidden pleasure and therefore a delight. Later they met at the Tea Room in Barrow's Stores, so they changed the name of their clique to the Barrovian Society. When Wiseman, who was editor of the school newspaper, printed a list of students who had excelled in some way, he noted that their group were "members of the T.C., B.S., etc."—and so they became the T.C.B.S. The nucleus of the group consisted of Ronald, Christopher, R.Q., and later Geoffrey Bache Smith. The members had diverse interests, which they shared with one another: Christopher favored math, natural sciences, and music; R.Q. enjoyed studying drawing and design, Renaissance painting, and the eighteenth century; Geoffrey was interested in "modern" (post-Chaucer) English studies and poetry. John Ronald, as his friends then called him, brought his passion for philology and mythology as well as his command of Germanic languages and Norse writings.

Ronald's interests were not all cerebral; he loved playing rugby, even though he suffered a broken nose that was never quite the same shape again. But most of his time not spent with the T.C.B.S. was spent in working at languages (his own as well as historical ones), debating, and studying for the scholarship exam. On December 17, 1910, he learned that he had won an award to study classics at Oxford. It was not a full scholarship, but with help from Father Francis and a fund at King Edward's, he would be able to go to the university.

He was even able to take a holiday that summer, after the final session at King Edward's. He and Hilary (who had left school to take up agriculture) were part of a group that toured Switzerland on foot. Just before returning to England, he bought some picture postcards, including one of a painting by J. Madelener called *Der Berggeist* ("the mountain spirit"). The picture shows an old man with a long white beard, flowing cape, and wide-brimmed hat with a white fawn nuzzling his hands. Tolkien kept the card, later writing on the cover he used to protect it, "Origin of Gandalf." He was back in England by early September, and a month later arrived at Oxford.

Money, as always, was a problem, but otherwise he was happy at Oxford. He joined the debating society and played rugby, and started his own club, the Apolausticks ("those devoted to self-indulgence"), which like the T.C.B.S. was a jolly group of male friends who loved to talk. He found himself bored by many of his studies, but discovered that the comparative philology professor was Joseph Wright—the same man who had written the Gothic primer that had so excited him years before. A scholar who had taught himself to read and write when he was fifteen (he had been working in woolen mills, not going to school, since he was six), Wright enjoyed a tremendous enthusiasm for philology, and knew enough to challenge Ronald in ways his other teachers could not.

Ronald found books on medieval Welsh and began to learn the language that had fascinated him since he had first seen the Welsh words on the sides of coal cars. At the same time, he began to draw and paint again, finding that he was gifted in drawing landscapes. His enthusiasm for languages did not abate, though; when he discovered Finnish, he said, "It quite intoxicated me." He began creating a language with strong Finnish elements; this would eventually become Quenya, or the High-elven tongue. As he began reading Finnish mythological poetry, he expressed his wish that English culture had retained more of "that very primitive undergrowth" of myth. It was a lack he would later rectify, as he created a complete new-old English mythology.

COMING OF AGE

Immediately on turning twenty-one, Ronald wrote Edith, declaring his love and asking how soon they could be married. To his dismay, she replied that she was engaged to be married to someone else.

Three years without communication, she explained, had persuaded her that he had probably forgotten her (as Father Francis had probably hoped); she was twenty-four and afraid she would be a spinster all her life if she did not accept the offer of George Field, who had been kind to her. But behind her words Ronald read her true message: that she would prefer to marry him. He took a train to Cheltenham. She met him at the station; and, after a day of walking and talking, Edith declared she would break off her engagement to George and marry Ronald.

This time, he did not keep his intentions from Father Francis; although the priest was no longer his guardian, he was still helping out financially, and the loss of that support would jeopardize his ability to continue his studies. Father Francis seemed resigned to the match, and made no objection. Oddly, Ronald had never mentioned Edith to his friends. As they decided to become formally betrothed, he informed his fellow T.C.B.S. members of the fact (but not of her name). They assured him that little would change among the group.

A greater danger to his studies was his late nights talking with his friends; Ronald found himself ill-prepared for his exams in Classics. He managed to pass Second Class, but the college noted that he had presented a practically flawless paper in comparative philology, due both to Joseph Wright's coaching and the fact that this was where Tolkien's greatest talents lay. The college suggested that since his strongest interests lay in the Germanic languages, such as Old and Middle English, he should consider transferring from Classics to the English School, which he did at the beginning of the 1913 summer term.

Now that he was studying what he really loved, he spent more time doing so. Even though he found his new field unexpectedly challenging, he delighted in Anglo-Saxon religious poetry and the Old Norse Eddas, with their magical repositories of Icelandic myth and legend.

The revived relationship with Edith, however, had hit a snag. While she was away, she had been happily active in the Church of England in Cheltenham. The Jessops, the family with whom she was staying, were staunchly anti-Catholic. While she was willing to convert to Catholicism, she did not want to provoke unpleasantness with her hosts; she said she would wait to renounce the Anglican Church until closer to the time of their marriage. But Ronald insisted that she immediately start attending a Catholic church; if her erstwhile friends persecuted her, he said, it would be just what had happened to his own mother, and thus not unexpected or devastating. Edith reluctantly acceded to his wishes. Just as she had feared, the Jessops reacted angrily, telling her to leave their home as soon as possible. She decided to share accommodations with her cousin, Jennie Grove.

On January 14, 1914, the first anniversary of Ronald and Edith's reunion, she was received into the Roman Catholic Church; shortly afterward, they were officially betrothed.

By late that summer, England had declared war on Germany, and young men across the country were enlisting to fight.

WORLD WAR I

If he managed to gain a First Class degree—and if he managed to survive the war—Ronald knew he would be able to find a good job in the academic world when the fighting was over. On the other hand, if he did not finish this final year and earn his degree, he might never be able to complete his college education. Fortunately, he discovered an army program that allowed him to begin training immediately while still leaving him enough time to finish his studies. He successfully won his First Class degree in June 1915. Shortly thereafter he joined his regiment, the Lancashire Fusiliers, which he had chosen because his friend Geoffrey Smith was a member. He was disappointed when they were assigned to different battalions.

After several months, as reports of the war's heavy casualties made them realize that he might not return from battle, Edith and Ronald decided not to wait until the war was over to wed. They were married March 22, 1916. She faced a moment of panic when she had to put her father's name and occupation on the marriage certificate; she had never told Ronald that she was illegitimate. When she told him later, he wrote her, "I think I love you even more tenderly because of all that, my wife," then said they should both simply forget it. On June 4, Ronald left for France and the Battle of the Somme.

At the end of the first day of fighting, R.Q. Gilson was among the twenty thousand Allied troops who had been killed. The horror of war surrounded the survivors, as life became a nightmare of marches and attacks, boredom interspersed with panic, mud, and dismembered, rotting corpses. During his time in France, Ronald developed little liking for the senior officers, but a great deal of respect for the privates, batmen (officers' servants), and noncommissioned officers of his battalion, who stolidly carried on under the most appalling circumstances. He wrote later that Sam Gamgee of *The Lord of the Rings* was based on "the English soldier, . . . the privates and batmen I knew in the 1914 war, and recognised as so far superior to myself."

Lice spread a disease called trench fever, which causes high fever, rash, headaches, and mental confusion. Ronald came down with the malady, and on November 8, 1916, he was shipped home to a Birmingham hospital. While he was recovering, he learned that Geoffrey Smith had been hit by fragments of a bursting shell and had died of complications of gangrene. Shortly before he was wounded, he had written Tolkien:

> My chief consolation is that if I am scuppered tonight . . . there will still be left a member of the great T.C.B.S. to voice what I dreamed and what we all agreed upon. For the death of one of its members cannot, I am determined, dissolve the T.C.B.S. . . . It cannot put an end to the immortal four! . . . May God bless you, my dear John Ronald, and may you say the things I have tried to say long after I am not there to say them, if such be my lot.

CREATING A NEW MYTHOLOGY

As Tolkien had been creating languages over the years, he had gradually come to realize that his languages must have a "history" in which to develop. He began his history, his mythological cycle, in a notebook on the cover of which he had written "The Book of Lost Tales." The stories he began here would eventually become *The Silmarillion.*

Humphrey Carpenter lists three reasons why Tolkien chose this time to begin his new mythology: Smith's letter; a desire, inspired by the T.C.B.S., to express himself in poetry (including prose poetry); and the wish to create a mythology for his native country. Surely the heightened sense of life engendered by battle had an effect, too, as did a note he received from the remaining one of the "immortal four," Christopher Wiseman, who wrote, "You ought to start the epic." And so he did.

He had time to write, for he spent much of the next two years in various hospitals. For a while, when he was on sick leave at Great Haywood in early 1917, Edith was able to join him. She helped by making a legible copy of the first story he wrote, "The Fall of Gondolin," and they spent their evenings playing the piano, reading poetry, and drawing.

They conceived a child during this respite from the war. When he was posted to Yorkshire, she followed him again, but after repeated transfers she and her cousin Jennie finally moved back to Cheltenham, where she had been happy during the three years of their separation. It was in a Cheltenham nursing home that their first son was born, on November 16, 1917. John Francis (for Father Francis) Reuel was a difficult labor. Edith nearly died, and suffered pain from the labor for many months afterward.

By now it seemed unlikely that Ronald would be sent back to the fighting, so Edith and John moved to Yorkshire to be near him. On his occasional leaves, they would wander together in a small nearby wood, where Edith would sing and dance for him. These precious days formed the basis of the central story of *The Silmarillion:* the mortal man Beren who falls in love with the immortal elven-maid Lúthien Tinúviel, first glimpsed dancing in a wood.

More than a half-century later, after Edith's death, Tolkien wrote to his son Christopher:

> She was (and knew she was) my Lúthien. I will say no more now. But I should like ere long to have a long talk with you. . . . Someone close in heart to me should know something about things that records do not record: the dreadful sufferings of our childhood, from which we rescued one another, but could not wholly heal wounds that later often proved disabling; the sufferings that we endured after our love began—all of which (over and above personal weaknesses) might help to make pardonable, or understandable, the lapses and darknesses which at times marred our lives—and to explain how these never touched our depths nor dimmed the memories of our youthful love.

A BRIEF STINT HELPING WRITE A DICTIONARY

During a period out of the hospital, in October 1918, Tolkien had gone to Oxford to see what employment prospects he might expect at the university when the war ended. The institution was in disarray and could offer little information, but while he was there he saw William Craigie, who had taught him Icelandic. Craigie was on the staff of the *Oxford New English Dictionary,* and he said he would be able to secure a position as assistant lexicographer for his former student. When the war ended the following month, Tolkien obtained permission to move to Oxford while he awaited official demobilization. By late November, he, Edith, baby John, and Jennie had moved into rooms near his new job, researching etymologies, or word origins (he began with *w: warm, wasp, water*). He later said of his stint on the dictionary staff, "I learned more in those two years than in any other equal period of my life." In later years, when he was chided for his spelling *dwarves* when the *OED* specified *dwarfs,* he rather grandiosely responded that he had *written* the *Oxford English Dictionary.*

Work on the dictionary was not expected to fill his entire day, nor to provide his entire income. He began to tutor students in Anglo-Saxon, and by the late summer of 1919 he and Edith could afford to rent a small house and hire a cook-housemaid. By the following spring, Ronald was earning enough from tuition to leave his job at the dictionary. Edith was pregnant again, and Ronald was making progress in his writing. When a position as reader (teacher) in English language became available at the University of Leeds, he applied, expecting nothing to come of it. Unexpectedly, he was awarded the position.

LEEDS

Unlike Oxford, Leeds was an industrial town whose smoke-stacks produced a thick fog of industrial pollutants. It was with some misgiving that he accepted the position and moved there, to the north of England. Edith stayed in Oxford to bear their second child, Michael Hilary Reuel, just as the October term began in Leeds. She remained in Oxford for several months, until early 1921.

Although Leeds was not as prestigious as Oxford, the head of the English Department nevertheless invited Tolkien to create a syllabus that would attract students to philology and give them a sound education in the field. Although the students in this Yorkshire town seemed much less lively than the friends he had cultivated in school, he was surprised and pleased to find that many of them were hard workers capable of achieving at a high level.

He was soon joined by a student he had tutored at Oxford, E.V. Gordon, now a junior lecturer in the language side of the Leeds English Department. The two men decided to compile an edition of the Middle English poem that had fascinated him earlier, *Sir Gawain and the Green Knight,* in an edition that would be suitable for college students. Gordon was industrious and Tolkien managed to keep up with him; their collaborative effort was published in 1925, when it was acknowledged as a major contribution to the study of medieval literature.

He also kept working on *The Book of Lost Tales / The Silmarillion,* but as he drew near the end, he turned to polishing and rewriting what he already had rather than finishing it. His career at Leeds continued to progress; he became a full professor in 1924 at the remarkably young age of thirty-two. That year, he and Edith bought a fairly large house surrounded by fields and had their third child, Christopher Reuel, named for Tolkien's friend Christopher Wiseman. Christopher Reuel Tolkien would grow up to edit his father's voluminous papers, including the posthumous twelve-volume *History of Middle-earth*.

Early in 1925, Tolkien learned that his old Icelandic teacher and Oxford dictionary coworker was moving to America; his position as professor of Anglo-Saxon at Oxford would soon be vacant. Tolkien applied for and won the position, and the family moved back to Oxford.

FINALLY SETTLING DOWN AT OXFORD

Humphrey Carpenter writes of this time,

> And after this, you might say, nothing else really happened. Tolkien came back to Oxford, was Rawlinson and Bosworth Professor of Anglo-Saxon for twenty years, was then elected Merton Professor of English Language and Literature, went to live in a conventional Oxford suburb where he spent the first part of his retirement, moved to a nondescript seaside resort, came back to Oxford after his wife died, and himself died a peaceful death at the age of eighty-one. . . . And that would be that—apart from the strange fact that during these years when "nothing happened" he wrote two books [*The Hobbit* and *The Lord of the Rings*] . . . that have captured the imagination and influenced the thinking of several million readers.

The Tolkiens settled into a comfortable house on Northmoor Road in 1926. In 1929, when their fourth child and first daughter, Priscilla Mary Reuel, was born, a larger house next door became available, and they decided to buy it. They moved in 1930, and finally stayed in one place until 1947.

In 1926 C.S. Lewis joined the English faculty. Tolkien invited him to join the Coalbiters, a group that met to read Icelandic sagas, and they soon began a long friendship. Lewis listened as Tolkien read from the manuscript of *The Silmarillion*, and urged him to complete it. Tolkien helped Lewis struggle with his religious doubts and explorations; when he explained his view of the story of Christ as a myth that had really happened, he helped Lewis find a new Christian faith. Lewis went on to write such overtly Christian writings as *The Screwtape Letters*, as well as the *Chronicles of Narnia* and many other works.

Lewis and Tolkien were two early members of the Inklings, a group that took the place of the Coalbiters once that group had finished reading all the principal Icelandic sagas. The original Inklings group was founded by an Oxford undergraduate, Tangye Lean, to bring together scholars to read and criticize unpublished manuscripts. When Lean left, the name stuck to a group of men, mostly dons at the university, who gathered around Lewis and met regularly. The Inklings were an early audience for Tolkien's readings from *The Hobbit* and *The Lord of the Rings*.

Tolkien had begun *The Hobbit* in 1930, as a story for his children, but abandoned it when they were no longer interested in an evening "story time." In 1936 a friend and a former student mentioned the manuscript to Susan Dagnall, a representative of publishers Allen and Unwin, who subsequently read it and encouraged him to finish it. Her enthusiasm was echoed by that of Rayner Unwin, the ten-year-old son of the publisher, who wrote a favorable report of it for his father. The book was published the following year, and was popular enough that publisher Stanley Unwin suggested he write a sequel. None of the stories he had already begun would do; they wanted more hobbits.

TOLKIEN'S EPIC IS PUBLISHED

It would be twelve years before he finished *The Lord of the Rings* in 1950. In a 1971 BBC radio interview, he recalled, "I remember I actually wept at the denouement." He went on to say, "But then of course there was a tremendous lot of revision," and he made a joke about errors that remained in the manuscript:

> I suppose I'm in a position where it doesn't matter what people think of me now—there were some frightful mistakes in grammar, which from a Professor of English Language and Lit are rather shocking. . . . There was one where I used *bestrode* as the past participle of *bestride!* [laughs]

In 1965, U.S. publisher Ace Books, taking advantage of a loophole in U.S. copyright laws, issued an unauthorized edition of *The Hobbit*, which sold especially well on college campuses. Rather than sue (Ace was legally able to refuse to pay Tolkien any royalties), the author started a quiet campaign pleading for "courtesy to living authors." The resultant outcry persuaded Ace to pay Tolkien a royalty for every copy sold and to promise not to print any more copies. This provided a boon for the authorized U.S. publisher, Ballantine, which profited by the attention and enthusiasm the Ace edition had stirred up.

With the success of *The Hobbit* and *The Lord of the Rings*, Tolkien could afford to retire from teaching and turn his attention to *The Silmarillion*—a daunting prospect, since he had been accumulating and revising it in bits and pieces for forty years. However, between attending to family obligations and responding to questions from readers all over the globe, he made little progress in bringing this massive project to fruition. He finally made an agreement with his youngest son that, should he die before completing the book, Christopher would complete it, a promise that eased his mind.

Tolkien was visiting friends in Bournemouth in late August 1973 when he became ill and was taken to the hospital. At first doctors felt he would recover from the acute bleeding gastric ulcer that had incapacitated him, but he developed a secondary infection and failed rapidly. He died at the age of eighty-one on September 2, 1973.

A SON'S PROMISES

Christopher Tolkien kept his promises to his father. Ronald was buried next to Edith. Their tombstones bear their names, birth and death years, and the names Ronald had given to his *Silmarillion* lovers: Lúthien on hers, Beren on his.

His larger promise—to edit and publish the mass of work his father left—has taken decades. A glance at this book's chronology for the years after Ronald's death will give an idea of the degree to which Christopher has devoted himself to fulfilling his father's plans and dreams.

CHAPTER 1

The Hobbit

READINGS ON

J.R.R. TOLKIEN

The Hobbit Is Rooted in the Tradition of Classic British Children's Novels

Lois R. Kuznets

In comparing *The Hobbit* to Lewis Carroll's *Alice's Adventures in Wonderland* and other works that are considered classic British children's novels, Lois Kuznets points out that Tolkien's work is rooted firmly in that great tradition. Authors of such classics deal similarly with time and space, use an obtrusive narrator, and create characters with whom children can identify. Kuznets, author of *When Toys Come Alive: Narratives of Animation, Metamorphosis, and Development*, has also written a study of Kenneth Grahame, whose *The Wind in the Willows* is often compared to Tolkien's writing.

If there is anything left to say about *The Hobbit*, it is this: no matter how Tolkien wished to deny it, to repudiate those very qualities that confirm it, his first novel is solidly based on the great tradition of the British children's classic.[1] For that reason above all, Tolkien's *The Hobbit*—like Lewis Carroll's *Alice's Adventures in Wonderland*, George Macdonald's *The Princess and the Goblin* and *The Princess and Curdie*, and Kenneth Grahame's *The Wind in the Willows*—still deserves critical consideration.

My aim here is to show how, in *The Hobbit*, in contrast to *The Lord of the Rings*, Tolkien employs a "rhetoric of childhood" highly influenced by these writers, Grahame and Macdonald in particular. I use the word "rhetoric" as Booth does in *The Rhetoric of Fiction*, to designate the means that the literary artist uses to persuade the reader to dwell, at least momentarily,

within a "realistic" or "fantastic" world totally created and controlled by the writer.[2] The writer exercises rhetorical control
largely through means technically known as voice (that is, point
of view or narrational stance), but also through style in general
as well as through choice of character, characterization, and
manipulation of time and space.

The classic rhetoric of childhood combines the following
characteristics: an obtrusive narrator, commenting, addressing the reader, and using richly descriptive prose;
characters with whom preadolescent children can comfort-
ably identify and who develop and change as they do; an
emphasis on the relationship between time and development within a compressed narrative time scheme; a circumscribed geography and a significant concern with the
security or danger of specific places in the setting.

I will discuss these rhetorical devices beginning with time
and space, moving on to the more problematic point of view
and associated stylistic matters, and ending with the com-
plexities of characterization and their implications.

TIME AND SPACE

The Hobbit covers about a year and emphasizes seasonal
change; movements in space are also correlated with
changes in season. Baggins, Thorin, and company make major changes in position on solstices and equinoxes. Simple
age-old seasonal associations are conventionally exploited:
spring is the time of hopeful starting out; summer signals
the ripening of adventure; autumn brings despair; winter is
total war and death; spring is peace and joyful return. Generally, in children's literature, seasons are also specifically
equated with developmental cycles: spring is associated
closely with growth and exploration of the outside world,
winter with a kind of hibernation or growth plateau. Sharing
this common pattern are the openings of *The Hobbit* and *The
Wind in the Willows*. Bilbo and Mole emerge from their respective holes in the spring of the year; they return only after much growth and development have taken place. Their
spring beginnings contrast with the autumn beginning of
The Fellowship of the Ring, which heralds another kind of
development in Frodo that leaves him without the impulse
ever again to respond to spring in Middle-earth.

The three-volume "interlaced" *Lord of the Rings*, covers
about one year too, but in *The Hobbit* Tolkien tells the story

straightforwardly and quickly, in digestible portions, with a feeling of some closure at the end of each incident. Children, like adults, are capable of delight in suspense and the unexpected, but they cannot for long patiently sustain a sense of incompleteness. Bilbo, in very childlike fashion, having already traveled for months, can hardly stand the short wait (in days) "on the doorstep"; child readers have barely a page of waiting before the light beams on the keyhole. As in this instance, children's literature both divides and compresses time and, therefore, good children's books are episodic despite their underlying unity.

Again in contrast with the trilogy, Tolkien's landscape in *The Hobbit* is a circumscribed bifurcated one with lowlands to the west and forested lands to the east of the central and longitudinal mountains and river. This spatial representation quite neatly divides the world into safe and dangerous sides. Grahame's geography in *The Wind in the Willows* is roughly similar, if less graphic; there the safe field and rich river cultures oppose the Wild Wood, which lies on the other side of The River. Such simple geography not only emblematically indicates outside good and evil but also represents inner states and relative psychic disturbance. So Mole is threatened and experiences sheer psychological "Terror of the Wild Wood" just as Bilbo and the dwarves experience Mirkwood. . . .

In the matter of maturing adventures underground, Carroll's *Alice* is the recognized children's literature exemplum and is, like *The Hobbit*, amenable to both Freudian and Jungian interpretation.[3] *The Hobbit* is also much like other children's classics in its depiction of this highly significant space. On the one hand, no one—certainly not Tolkien—beats Grahame in the detailed description of what one might call the secure "domestic underground": comfortable accommodations for gentlemen of limited (Mole) and extensive (Badger) means.[4] On the other hand, Macdonald shares with Tolkien a fascination with the dangerous "foreign underground": the wonder of mountain caves, their terrors, treasures, and the characteristics of their degenerate inhabitants. The following passage, for instance, is part of Macdonald's long introductory description of the "beautiful terror" of mountains: "But the inside, who shall tell what lies there? Caverns of the awfullest solitude, their walls miles thick, sparkling with ores of gold or silver, copper or iron, tin or mercury, studded perhaps with precious stones—perhaps a brook, with eyeless fish in it, running, running ceaselessly, cold and babbling, through banks crusted with carbuncles and golden topazes, or over a gravel of which some of the stones are rubies and emeralds, perhaps diamonds and sapphires—who can tell?"[5]

As Robert Wolff points out in his study of Macdonald, this passage from *The Princess and Curdie* (1882) and others like it from the totally cave-oriented *The Princess and the Goblin* (1871) closely resemble the writings of the nineteenth-century German Romantics Novalis, Hoffmann, and Tieck.[6] Tolkien's cave descriptions, both in *The Hobbit* and in *The Lord of the Rings*, belong to a long literary line which Macdonald, not Tolkien, introduced into children's literature. Tolkien does, however, combine and relate the safe with the dangerous undergrounds as Grahame and Macdonald do not.

NARRATIVE VOICE

In point of view as in use of time and space Tolkien, in *The Hobbit*, belongs with these writers. The rhetorical element that distinguishes *The Hobbit* most immediately from his later books, is the obtrusive narrator. In *The Hobbit*, the narrator is constantly addressing the reader and is thus involved in a kind of "talking to children," as Tolkien himself regretfully points out.[7] This is, indeed, the most usual voice in all the great classics of British children's literature. A rhetorical convention like any other, the obtrusive narrative voice can be used well or badly. When it is well used, the voice can steer the child along the course of a complicated narrative, Socratically raise certain questions in his or her mind, and point to implications beneath the surface of behavior or events. Abused, it can be cloyingly didactic.

In the work of better children's writers, the obtrusive narrator is the instrument of emotional sensitivity, moral perception, and playfulness. Lewis Carroll is working within this convention when he writes: "'Well!' thought Alice to herself, 'after such a fall as this, I shall think nothing of tumbling downstairs. How brave they'll all think me at home! Why I wouldn't say anything about it even if I fell off the top of the house.' (Which was very likely true.)"[8] C.S. Lewis, who readily admits the influence of the rhetoric of childhood, also uses that convention. He writes, in *The Lion, the Witch and the Wardrobe*, after the sacrifice of Aslan: "I hope no one who reads this book has been quite as miserable as Susan and Lucy were that night; but if you have been—if you've been up all night and cried till you have no more tears left in you—you will know that there comes in the end a sort of quietness. You feel as if nothing was ever going to happen again."[9] Tolkien uses it particularly skillfully when he comments dryly, "You are familiar with Thorin's style on important occasions, so I will not give you any more of it, though he went on a good deal longer than this" (p. 203), or notes about Bilbo's approach to the dragon's lair: "Going on from there was the bravest thing he ever did. The tremendous things that happened afterwards were as nothing compared to it. He fought the real battle in the tunnel alone, before he ever saw the vast danger that lay in wait" (pp. 225f.).

The continued practice of reading aloud to children partly accounts for the persistence of the obtrusive narrator, with its explicitly oral quality. But this convention has always been more than just mechanical; it can be a special gift from adult author to child reader. The obtrusive narrator implicitly promises protection and companionship even when one is reading alone (or when childlike characters are left without protectors like Gandalf). One trusts the voice, at least, to desert neither the characters nor the reader, to say when one should be afraid and therefore alert and prudent and when one—either character or reader—can safely venture on or lay oneself down to sleep. This voice is the voice of a benevolent anthropomorphic god—not only the creator but the guardian of the imaginary universe in which it persuades the reader to dwell. . . .

SENSORY DETAIL

Other aspects of Tolkien's style . . . reveal that the rhetoric of childhood did not come as naturally or as richly to him as to some of his predecessors. Particularly noticeable to the reader of other great children's books is Tolkien's lack of sensory detail. In *The Hobbit*, characters like to eat but when they get a chance to do so they never seem to taste or smell their food; it's all dreams of bacon and eggs. Contrast Tolkien's eating dreams or scenes with Grahame's evocative prose: "When the girl returned, some hours later, she carried a tray, with a cup of fragrant tea steaming on it; and a plate piled up with very hot buttered toast, cut thick, very brown on both sides, with butter running through the holes in it in great golden drops, like honey from the honeycomb. The smell of that buttered toast simply talked to Toad."[10] The visually intriguing sport of smoking pipes and blowing smoke rings is conveyed by Tolkien with far more reality as an oral satisfaction than is eating. The sense of touch, exploited by Macdonald and C.S. Lewis after him is not indulged; sensory discomforts—with which children are unfortunately very familiar—are mentioned but minimized.

Tolkien thought of himself as having "a very strong visual imagination" that was "not so strong in other points." He revealingly doubted "if many authors visualize very closely faces and voices."[11] This suggests not only that lack of sensory imagination already noted but also the nature of Tolkien's visual imagination: he doesn't see things close up very clearly—unlike many children and writers for children—but has a much longer visual span; he is able to reproduce total landscapes and see relationships among landmarks; he is basically uninterested in interior or decorative details. Tolkien is figuratively farsighted rather than nearsighted.

Tolkien's lack of sensory detail and his long view are not particularly characteristic of the rhetoric of childhood, but in other stylistic matters, he is again among the masters. In *The Hobbit*, there is plenty of one thing Carroll's Alice wanted: "conversation." Characters talk to each other naturally and with differentiation among their speech patterns. They do not make speeches much or tell seemingly interminable "digressive" tales, as they are wont to do in the trilogy. They also make up words, like "bebother" and "confustication," and use constructions like "miserabler" as Carroll does. They engage in verbal trickery and combat, riddle games, and raillery—remnants of ancient verbal pastimes that also appear in Macdonald's and Carroll's works. Neither of the latter has characters play the riddle game as straightforwardly as Tolkien does in the Gollum chapter; however, Macdonald's Curdie taunts the goblins in much the same way that Bilbo taunts the spiders in Mirkwood. Another of Macdonald's characters, Diamond in *At the Back of the North Wind*, brings back poetry from other worlds and spiritual experiences, inspired in a Caedmonian fashion [Caedmon: 7th-century Anglo-Saxon poet], as many of Tolkien's characters are. The general interspersion of verse and song in the prose narrative is another remnant of an earlier tradition that has remained longer in children's fiction than in adult and is exploited by all of the authors mentioned. Tolkien's most original touch in the matter of dialogue and the like is to have Gollum talk the true "rhetoric of children," narcissistic baby talk; one wonders whether children don't catch on to this faster than adults.

CHARACTERS AND RELATIONSHIPS

The physical and emotional traits of Tolkien's characters and the relationships among them are well within the rhetoric of childhood. The invention of the beardless, three-to-four-foot-tall hobbit is especially so. In beardlessness, and size (roughly the height of the four-to-seven-year-old child), the hobbit evokes the most primitive type of identification on the part of children. Children's literature abounds with characters from Tom Thumb to Alice whose size is in some fashion contrasted with the demands of the world around them. These characters have, in various ways, to use the power of the psyche to overcome or to take advantage of the limits of their physical power (which is reflected, on a deeper level, by the male characters' lack of a beard).

Significantly, the other notable characteristic of the hobbits, their hairy feet, is virtually ignored in the trilogy. These feet symbolize a relationship to the animal kingdom that often appears in children's literature—where childlike characters are animals, or where children have special relationships with animals from whom they receive uncritical affection and toward whom they can feel superior and grown-up. The hobbits' hairy feet are, however, a vestigial trait related to much less conscious identification with animals on the part of children. Bettelheim, in *The Uses of Enchantment*, describes a whole cycle of animal transformation stories as having a repulsion-recognition-integration theme, through which the child first tries to rid himself of his "animal" instincts, especially sexuality, then recognizes them as part of himself, and finally integrates them into his personality and so controls them.[12] The hobbits' hairy feet are constant reminders of both the good and bad aspects of one's relationship to animals; hairy feet are somewhat repulsive but also allow more freedom of self-expression than even bare feet do. The child in me is both repelled by the grotesquerie and attracted to the freedom of those hairy feet. After all, to wear shoes is one of the continuing restraints and privileges of being grown-up and "civilized."

The hobbit species is truly an original and inspired sub-creation. Certain other creatures or features seem less original when one compares, for example, Tolkien's wily chatty dragon with Grahame's "reluctant dragon." And Gollum of *The Hobbit* is preceded by strange, degenerate animal creatures that live in the caves of Macdonald's *The Princess and the Goblin* and *The Princess and Curdie.* The conception of physical and moral degeneration of both species and individuals living away from fresh air and light is also a prominent theme of the two *Princess* books. Macdonald too uses savior birds and in the great battle at the end of *The Princess and Curdie* a battalion of pigeons rescues the outnumbered forces of good.[13]

The character of the hero or heroine is a central issue in the rhetoric of childhood. In contrast to Frodo [in *The Lord of the Rings*], Bilbo is the typical hero of children's literature with the typical quest. Bilbo and Frodo are exactly the same age at the beginning of their respective quests, but Bilbo is youthful and inexperienced, Frodo much more mature and relatively learned. In addition, the nature of Frodo's quest is not to find himself but to lose himself and so to find himself on another, other-worldly level. Self-integration of Bilbo's type, not self-transcendence of Frodo's type, is *the* quest of children's literature.

RELATIONSHIP BETWEEN THE HERO AND THE CHILD

More specifically, Bilbo, like many heroes of children's literature, displays all the outer traits and needs of the period that Freud designates as latency, when Oedipal and sexual conflicts are temporarily at rest. This period corresponds roughly to the elementary-school years. Erikson identifies it as the "fourth age of man" in which the main conflict is one between "industry and inferiority." This is the period when the child must learn the "fundamentals of technology" and become "ready to handle the utensils, the tools, and weapons used by the big people."[14] That is, among other things, what Bilbo is doing: discovering that he has not only inner resources but outer skills—seeing clearly, moving quietly, throwing stones, as well as developing power to wield the sword—that make it possible for him to function in a world less protected than his home.

The break at that particular period of life from home to public school was the most significant trauma for many an

English schoolboy, as we see not only in adult memoirs but in children's literature of the schoolboy variety (slang from which sometimes surfaces in the prose of *The Hobbit*). The struggle to become one of the boys is present in *The Hobbit* although not so blatantly as in these realistic novels.

Present too, in the fantasy element of the work, is the desire to *repress* rather than express competitive conflict and much of the other psychological conflict of childhood. This repression is characteristic of another kind of children's book: Lili Peller, a child psychologist, calls it "the early tale." The stories that she so designates have in common a denial of conflicts inherent in the dichotomies of male-female, old-young. She notes: "In each story we find a group of loyal friends and we find a Protector who can work magic.... Every member of the group has unique gifts and skills and foibles.... The magician-Protector stays offstage or near the wing and the friends' actions and their feelings really carry the story.... Family relations of all kinds are nonexistent or they are at the very fringe of the story.... Most of them [the characters] belong to different species. Who will compare a monkey with a toad?"[15] Tolkien's story exhibits many of the repressive elements of "the early tale." One might note especially here the absence of contact with "the opposite sex"—a trait that *The Hobbit* shares with the major portion of *The Wind in the Willows*. Without reference to the clear misogyny of *The Lord of the Rings*, even a feminist might find Bilbo, as a character in *The Hobbit*, androgynous rather than misogynous in his bachelorhood. Either male or female children may, therefore, finally come to identify with him.[16]

BILBO'S DEVELOPMENT

One element of Peller's early tale that Tolkien does not replicate is a static quality in terms of the growth and development of the characters. This growth and development in Bilbo is the major theme of the story. But what Tolkien regarded as the end product of that growth and development in 1937 is quite different from what he tried to make it later, by changing the Gollum chapter after he began the trilogy.[17] In the early version, the high point of Bilbo's moral development can only be construed as an expanded concept of *justice* that goes beyond selfish desires to acknowledge Bard's claims: "Now these were fair words and true, if proudly and grimly spoken; and Bilbo thought that Thorin would at once admit what justice was in them" (p. 275).

Bilbo's subsequent renunciation of the Arkenstone perhaps foreshadows his later renunciation of the ring but is well within the morality of fairness and sharing inculcated in children at an early age. This morality is synonymous with justice to them; therefore, a child might be capable of what Bilbo is capable of at the high point of his moral development in *The Hobbit.*

Mercy, however, is not a concept of childhood, as many, including Tolkien himself, have been at pains to point out.[18] Tolkien attempted to write the concept of mercy into Bilbo's development when he revised *The Hobbit* in the 1950s. The moment in "Riddles in the Dark" when Bilbo has a flash of understanding of Gollum's fallen state—"a glimpse of endless unmarked days without light or hope of betterment, hard stone, cold fish, sneaking and whispering" (p. 78)—is not part of the original story nor of the usual rhetoric of childhood.

The "mercy passage" is really connected with the very unchildlike sacrificial development of Frodo's personality and his acknowledgment of his relationship to "it," his shadow, Gollum. In *The Lord of the Rings*, Frodo practically goes mad and the three small creatures—Frodo, Gollum, and Sam—who move across the devastated landscape are emblematic not only of man's state in general, but also of the struggle in the divided psyche among superego, id, and ego.[19] Sam, the ego figure, survives, but he is not, after all, prominent even among the several "heroes" of the narrative.[20]

Bilbo's resourcefulness and basic sanity are honored in *The Hobbit*, not overshadowed by saintliness, as Sam's similar qualities are in the trilogy. The contrast between Bilbo and Frodo as heroes recalls Chesterton's distinction: "In the fairy tales, the cosmos goes mad, but the hero does not go mad. In the modern novels, the hero is mad before the book begins and suffers from the harsh steadiness and cruel sanity of the cosmos."[21] In most good children's literature, as in fairy tales, the hero or heroine appears to represent the healthy developing ego with its capacity for just action and for survival in *this* world. Bilbo lives. And Bilbo joins Alice, Curdie, Mole, Rat, and Toad in the gallery of such sane and down-to-earth protagonists. In this way, as in others, *The Hobbit* belongs to the great tradition of "the rhetoric of childhood."

Notes

Note: Unless otherwise indicated, quotations from *The Hobbit* are from the Houghton Mifflin edition (Boston, 1938).

1. In an early foreword to *The Fellowship of the Ring*, Tolkien seems to concede that *The Hobbit* was composed for his children: "Since my children and others of their age, who first heard of the Ring, have grown older with the years, this book speaks more plainly of the darker things which lurked only on the borders of the earlier tale" (New York: Ace Books, n.d.), p. 9. In a late interview with Philip Norman, Tolkien denies that *The Hobbit* is a children's book and repudiates "anything that in any way was marked out in 'The Hobbit' as for children instead of just for people." "The Prevalence of Hobbits," *New York Times Magazine*, Jan. 15, 1967, p. 100.

   This is in clear contrast to C.S. Lewis who chose the children's story because it was "the best art-form" for those things he had to say. Lewis, "Three Ways of Writing for Children," in *Of Other Worlds, Essays and Stories*, ed. Walter Hooper (New York, 1966), p. 23.

2. Wayne Booth, *The Rhetoric of Fiction* (Chicago, 1961).

3. The most famous of these analyses of Alice is William Empson's "The Child as Swain" in *Some Versions of Pastoral* (New York, 1950). Randel Helms does the same for *The Hobbit* in "The Hobbit as Swain," *Tolkien's World* (Boston, 1974), pp. 41–55. See also Dorothy Matthews, "The Psychological Journey of Bilbo Baggins" in *A Tolkien Compass*, ed. Jared Lobdell (La Salle, Ill., 1975), pp. 29–42, and Marion Zimmer Bradley, "Men, Halflings and Hero-Worship," in *Tolkien and the Critics*, ed. Neil D. Isaacs and Rose A. Zimbardo (Notre Dame, Ind., 1968), pp. 109–27.

4. We are introduced to Badger's home thus: "He shuffled on in front of them, carrying the light and they followed him, nudging each other in an anticipating sort of way, down a long, gloomy, and to tell the truth, decidedly shabby passage, into a sort of central-hall, out of which they could dimly see other long tunnel-like passages mysterious and without apparent end. But there were doors in the hall as well—stout oaken comfortable looking doors. One of these Badger flung open, and at once they found themselves in all the glow and warmth of a large fire-lit kitchen." Another paragraph is devoted to describing that kitchen, ending with: "The ruddy brick floor smiled up at the smoky ceiling; the oaken settles, shiny with long wear, exchanged cheerful glances with each other; plates on the dresser grinned at pots on the shelf, and the merry fire-

light flickered and played over everything without distinction." Kenneth Grahame, *The Wind in the Willows* (1908; rpt. New York, 1969), pp. 58–59.

5. Macdonald, *The Princess and Curdie* (1882; rpt. London, 1964), p. 11. Sharing my sense of Tolkien's debt to Macdonald in this and other ways are both Hugh Crago and Robert L. Wolff. See Crago, "Remarks on the Nature and Development of Fantasy," in J.S. Ryan, *Tolkien: Cult or Culture?* (Armidale, Australia, 1969), Appendix D, esp. pp. 216–20, and Wolff, *The Golden Key: A Study of the Fiction of George Macdonald* (New Haven, Conn., 1961), p. 9.

6. Wolff, pp. 170–71.

7. Tolkien says, "'The Hobbit' was written in what I should now regard as a bad style, as if one were talking to children." Norman, p. 100.

8. Carroll, *Alice's Adventures in Wonderland* (1865; rpt. Baltimore, Md., 1946), p. 25.

9. Lewis, *The Lion, the Witch and the Wardrobe* (New York, 1950), p. 128.

10. Grahame, p. 135.

11. Norman, p. 102.

12. Bettelheim, *The Uses of Enchantment: The Meaning and Importance of Fairy Tales* (1975; rpt. New York, 1977), pp. 227–310 and passim.

13. Tolkien's very use of the word "goblin" in *The Hobbit*, which he changes to "orc" in the trilogy (and in his revision of the Gollum chapter), perhaps subconsciously reflects his debt to Macdonald.

14. Erik H. Erikson, "The Eight Ages of Man," *Childhood and Society*, 2nd ed. (New York, 1963), pp. 247–74, esp. 258–60. Bilbo also at first resembles the third son or "Dummy" in fairy tales that Bettelheim analyzes, p. 75.

15. Peller, "Daydreams and Children's Favorite Books," in *The Causes of Behavior*, 2nd ed., ed. Judy F. Rosenblith and Wesley Allinsmith (Boston, 1970), pp. 469–75.

16. Bettelheim claims that for children the sex of the protagonist comes not to matter, p. 59.

17. For an analysis of the changes Tolkien made in *The Hobbit* see Bonniejean Christensen, "Gollum's Character Transformation in *The Hobbit*," *Tolkien Compass*, ed. Lobdell, pp. 9–28.

18. Tolkien, "On Fairy-Stories," p. 44. See also Bettelheim, p. 144.

19. Compare Tolkien's portrayal of the Frodo-Gollum-Sam struggles with Freud's description of the close relationship between the Superego and the Id and of the Ego's struggles to serve, mediate, and temper both their excesses while developing and strengthening itself in relation to the outside world. See Sigmund Freud, *The Ego and the Id*, trans. Joan Rivière (New York, 1960).
20. Merry and Pippin come closest to being children's heroes.
21. G.K. Chesterton, "The Dragon's Grandmother," *Tremendous Truths* (New York, 1927), p. 126.

Adult Themes in a Tale to Be Read to Children

Paul H. Kocher

Although *The Hobbit* uses such child-pleasing devices as direct address and sound effects meant to be read aloud, Tolkien treats several issues that can only be comprehended by adults, writes Paul H. Kocher. Although the story is suitable for children, it operates throughout at two separate levels of maturity. Besides *Master of Middle-earth: The Fiction of J.R.R. Tolkien* (from which this essay is excerpted) and a book on Tolkien's *The Silmarillion*, Kocher has also written on Elizabethan England and Christopher Marlowe.

The beginning of wisdom in understanding *The Hobbit* is to think of Tolkien, or another adult, in a chair by the fireside telling the story to a semicircle of children sitting on the floor facing him. From the opening paragraphs hardly a page goes by in which the narrator does not address the children directly in the first person singular. Since the breed of hobbits has just sprung freshly minted from his brain, he loses no time in telling his young listeners about how they look and behave, notably their shyness "when large stupid folk like you and me come blundering along," and he ends his description by, "Now you know enough to go on with. As I was saying. . . ."[1] Sometimes he uses the direct address technique to create anticipation, as in introducing Gandalf: "Gandalf! If you had heard only a quarter of what I have heard about him, and I have only heard very little of all there is to hear, you would be prepared for any sort of remarkable tale." Sometimes his remarks to the child audience take on a genial, joking tone, as in pointing out the flaw in Bilbo's

---

1. All references are to *The Hobbit* (Boston: Houghton Mifflin Co., 1967).

plan for freeing the captive dwarves by putting them into barrels (his inability to put himself into one): "Most likely you saw it some time ago and have been laughing at him; but I don't suppose you would have done half as well yourselves in his place." Then, there are jocular interjections of no special moment, but aimed at maintaining a playful intimacy: "If you want to know what *cram* is, I can only say that I don't know the recipe; but it is biscuitish. . . ."

Tolkien also makes the technique work for him expositorily in making clear to the youngsters important shifts in the plot sequence. Normally he describes every scene from Bilbo's point of view, and describes none in which Bilbo himself is not present. But Chapter XIV diverges to report what happened at Lake-town, while Bilbo and the dwarves were shut inside Erebor, when Smaug the dragon attacked the town and was killed by Bard the archer. So Tolkien opens the chapter with the sentence: "Now if you wish, like the dwarves, to hear news of Smaug, you must go back again to the evening when he smashed the door and flew off in a rage, two days before." Incidentally, this careful score-keeping of days elapsed at every stage of his tale is typical of Tolkien. Having narrated events at Lake-town he steers his young audience back to their hero with the words, "Now we will return to Bilbo and the dwarves." And, on occasion, in order to remind them of an important fact, already explained some time before, which they may have forgotten, he repeats it. Thus when the Master in Lake-town judges Thorin's claim to the treasure by inheritance to be a fraud Tolkien reiterates what Gandalf and Elrond acknowledged earlier: "He was wrong. Thorin, of course, was really the grandson of the king under the Mountain. . . ." This care in keeping the plot crystal clear is adapted to the possible squirmings and short attentiveness of the children he is speaking to.

DEVICES AIMED AT A YOUNG AUDIENCE

Also for their benefit is Tolkien's method all through *The Hobbit* of prefacing the introduction into the story of each new race with a paragraph or so setting forth in plain words whatever needs to be known about its looks, its habits, its traits, and whether it is good or bad. He has started this practice off with the hobbits. He extends it to trolls, dwarves, goblins, eagles, elves, and lakemen as each of these makes its entry. These little capsules of racial qualities are enlivened usually with personal interjections: "Yes, I am afraid trolls do behave like that, even those with only one head each"; or "Eagles are not kindly birds," but they did come to the rescue of Bilbo's party, and "a very good thing too!" Goblins are wicked and bear a special grudge against dwarves "because of the war which you have heard mentioned, but which does not come into this tale." Elves are hunters by starlight at the edges of the wood and are "Good People." After such set pieces no small auditor will be in any doubt as to which people he should cheer for. The whole tale gives him a very firm moral framework by which to judge.[2]

Another minor but persistent device in the manner of its telling likewise is meant to delight childish ears. The prose is full of sound effects, which the eye of the reader might miss but the hearing of the listener would not. Bilbo's doorbell rings *ding-dong-a-ling-dang;* Gandalf's smoke rings go *pop!;* the fire from his wand explodes with a *poof;* Bombur falls out of a tree *plop* onto the ground; Bilbo falls *splash!* into the water, and so on at every turn. Nor are these sound effects limited to the prose. Many of the poems are designed more for onomatopoeic purposes than for content. One prime example is the song of the goblins underground after their capture of Bilbo and the dwarves, with its *Clash, crash! Crush, smash!* and *Swish, smack! Whip crack* and *Ho, ho, my lad.* The elves' barrel-rolling song has all the appropriate noises, from *roll-roll-rolling* to *splash plump!* and *down they bump!* Tolkien knows that up to a certain age children like their stories to be highly audible.[3]

But the question as to what age Tolkien is addressing cannot be long deferred. Probably he himself had no precise answer in mind, but the very nature of the tale and the methods of its telling draw the principal parameters. The children listening to its recital must be young enough not to resent the genial fatherliness of the I-You technique, the encapsulated expositions, sound effects, and the rest, yet old enough

2. Only in the very last paragraph does Tolkien attach this limited framework to a wider cosmic order, foreshadowing the ideas discussed in the next chapter, as Gandalf asks Bilbo laughingly: "Surely you don't disbelieve the prophecies, because you had a hand in bringing them about yourself? You don't really suppose, do you, that all your adventures and escapes were managed by mere luck, just for your sole benefit?" This reference is too fleeting to affect the atmosphere of the tale as a whole and would not, I suppose, mean much to children. 3. On one or two occasions Tolkien's choice of similes is obviously dictated by children's interests: Bilbo laughs at the dwarf Fili wrapped around with spider webs "jerking his stiff arms and legs as he danced on the spider-string under his armpits, just like one of those funny toys bobbing on a wire." But his atrocious punning in describing the origins of the game of golf seems destined for the unlucky ears of adults.

to be able to cope with the fairly stiff vocabulary used on many occasions and to make at least something of the maturer elements that keep cropping up in what they hear. For, although *The Hobbit* is predominantly juvenile fiction, it is not all of a piece. Much of the confusion about it arises from the fact that it contains episodes more suited to the adult mind than the child's.

EPISODES FOR ADULT MINDS

One such is Bard's claim to a share in Smaug's treasure after he has killed the dragon, a claim made not only on his own behalf but also on behalf of the elves and the people of Lake-town. Tolkien has built up here a very pretty conundrum in law, equity, and morals. The treasure consists of a hoard gathered by Thorin's ancestors, but Smaug has mingled with it unestimated valuables belonging to Bard's forebears in the city of Dale. So Bard has a clear legal claim to some unclear fraction. The Lake-town men have no title in law to any portion but rest their case on the argument that Thorin owes them an equitable share because the dwarves roused Smaug to destroy their town, leaving them now destitute; and besides they helped to outfit the dwarf expedition when it was penniless. Bard invokes for them, in fact, the general principle that the wealthy "may have pity beyond right on the needy that befriended them when they were in want." And what of the elves' contention that the dwarves stole the treasure from them in the first place, as against the dwarf reply that they took it in payment for goldsmith work for the elves under a contract which their king later refused to honor? A Solomon might well pick his way gingerly among these claims and counterclaims, especially when faced with Thorin's answer that he is not responsible for Smaug's devastations, and will not bargain under threat of siege by an army anyway. If so, what is even the wise child to make of it all?

Well, Tolkien does not leave his audience, young or old, without some guidance. He comes right out and says of Bard's claim when first uttered, "Now these were fair words and true, if proudly and grimly spoken; and Bilbo thought that Thorin would at once admit what justice was in them." Thorin's refusal is characterized as dwarfish "lust" for gold fevered by brooding on the dragon's hoard. The experienced reader of Tolkien's other writings recognizes here his usual condemnation of the cardinal sin of "possessiveness," which besets dwarves as a race and which indeed is at the core of all the evil underlying the War of the Ring, and much other ill in the world besides. But Bard is a little too eager to resort to arms, being himself somewhat afflicted by the same curse. He has to be rebuked by the elf king, who contrives to conquer the same inclination to greed in his own breast, "Long will I tarry, ere I begin this war for gold. . . . Let us hope still for something that will bring reconciliation." Bilbo tries to break the deadlock by setting a moral example, but one which, oddly, requires an initial act of theft. After hiding in his pocket the great jeweled Arkenstone he steals from the recovered treasure, on the theory that it represents the one-fourteenth share promised him by the dwarves, Bilbo carries it secretly to Bard's camp by night, gives it to him freely to use as a bargaining counter against Thorin, and returns to the dwarves inside the mountain to face the music. For all this he is highly praised by Gandalf, surely a spokesman for Tolkien. Bilbo's self-sacrifice does not work out as planned, however, and open war between the contestants for Smaug's gold is averted only by the unforeseen attack of an army of goblins, which unites them against the common enemy. Tolkien's solution of the complex problem of ownership is finally moral. It comes about through the dying Thorin's repentance for his greed, which leads his followers to a generous sharing of the hoard with their new friends. This strongly fortifies the moral tone of the adventure, which began sordidly enough from motives of profit and revenge. But a good deal of rather adult territory has to be traversed to reach this consummation. One wonders what most child auditors would get out of it beyond the general impression that it is wrong to fight over who owns what. In this climactic spot the story really operates at two separate levels of maturity.

A similar double track seems to run through that other critical episode of Bilbo's encounter with Gollum in the tunnels under the goblin mountain. The riddle game the two play would be fun for audiences of any age, as its prototype was in Norse and Anglo-Saxon literature. But the case may well be otherwise when it comes to the portrayal of Gollum's character, with its mixture of cruelty, greed, and miserable loneliness, and Bilbo's response of horror, fear, and pity. Taken alone, any one of these emotions is as familiar to a child as to his parents, but their skillful blending as achieved by Tolkien requires some sophistication of understanding, which comes only with years. Particularly the pity that causes Bilbo to spare the life of a vile creature whom he hates and fears seems a high moral quality of which Tolkien writes, over the heads of all save a mature audience: "A sudden understanding, a pity mixed with horror, welled up in Bilbo's heart: a glimpse of endless unmarked days without light or hope of betterment. . . ." Tolkien is already looking ahead to that scene of revelation in *The Lord of the Rings* in which Gandalf tells Frodo that Bilbo's compassion in sparing Gollum would later save the world. However that may be, in *The Hobbit* the whole episode is one more example to Tolkien's writing at the same time both for children and for the parents who will often be reading them the tale. A fair enough practice, provided it can be so managed as not to confuse or irritate both parties.

SLY DIGS AT MODERN LIFE

Plenty of other passages of the same double character come readily to mind, frequently in the form of sly hits by Tolkien at some favorite targets in modern life. He pokes fun, for instance, at the stodgy respectability of hobbit (or human) society which brands as "queer" any hobbit who travels to foreign parts or has even mildly unusual experiences. The family of such a black sheep always hastens to hush up the offense. Finding himself "no longer quite respectable" on his return from his adventure, Bilbo "took to writing poetry and visiting the elves." Whereupon his neighbors thought him mad. Tolkien laughs at this same rationalistic rejection of fantasy again in the Lake-town episode when he writes that "some young people in the town openly doubted the existence of any dragon in the mountain, and laughed at the greybeards and gammers who said that they had seen him flying in the sky in their younger days"—this despite the fact that Smaug is snoring on his hoard not many miles to the north. Or, another shaft at modern skeptical materialism: ". . . one morning long ago in the quiet of the world, when there was less noise and more green, and the hobbits were still numerous and prosperous. . . ." Or, more plainly still, Tolkien's usual vendetta against our machine age showing through his remarks about goblins, that they love wheels and engines: "It is not unlikely that they invented some of the machines that have since troubled the world, especially the ingenious devices for killing large numbers of people at once," but in Bilbo's day "they had not advanced (as it is called) so far." Tolkien was ecologist, champion of the extraordinary, hater of "progress," lover of handicrafts, detester of war long before such attitudes became fashionable.

Besides the paramount interest *The Hobbit* can claim in its own right as the earliest specimen of Tolkien's fiction to be published and therefore as showing his art in its infancy, it has also great interest as the immediate precursor—and, to some extent, source—of the far more finished *Lord of the Rings.* In the Foreword to the latter work Tolkien describes *The Hobbit* as being drawn irresistibly toward the materials he had been assembling for several years past to tell the history of the earlier Ages of Middle-earth. So much so that glimpses crept into it "unbidden of things higher or deeper or darker than its surface: Durin, Moria, Gandalf, the Necromancer, the Ring.". . .

THE RING: LINK BETWEEN *THE HOBBIT* AND *THE LORD OF THE RINGS*

Of special import is the use Tolkien makes of the Ring he first described in *The Hobbit* as a prize won by Bilbo from Gollum in the riddle contest. Judging by the text of that story as a whole, Tolkien originally thought of the Ring only as one of those rings of invisibility that abound in fairy tales, wonder-working but harmless. Bilbo puts it on his finger and takes it off frequently as a means of escape from dangers that threaten him from time to time in caves, forests, dungeons, and battles. Yet it does not enslave him or impair his moral outlook in the slightest. On the contrary, he has become a stronger and better hobbit by the time the story ends. After this first version had been completed Tolkien began writing *The Lord of the Rings* as a sequel and only then, it seems, conceived of the scheme of taking over Bilbo's Ring and turning it into the potent instrument of evil around which swirls all the action of the epic. Bilbo's finding of it, which in *The Hobbit* is merely a turning point in his personal "career," was to be magnified into a turning point in the history of Middle-earth. The Ring itself, which *The Hobbit* does not report as belonging to the Necromancer or anybody else, was to be attributed to Sauron as maker and master, in order to account for its malignant power over anyone wearing it.

The Ring, therefore, is the link that inseparably binds the later epic to the earlier children's story. But how to explain the glaring differences between Bilbo's harmless little gold band and Sauron's ruling Ring on which hung the fate of the world? Tolkien does not really try to explain them in any detail, but he does give some hints to pacify the curious reader. In the section of his Prologue to the second (1965) edition of the epic, titled "Of the Finding of the Ring," Tolkien remarks that Bilbo had not told his friends the true story of how he obtained the Ring and that Gandalf had long suspected the falsehood. Such a lapse on the part of a usually truthful hobbit struck Gandalf as very "strange and suspicious" and made him begin to doubt that the Ring was the innocent plaything it seemed on the surface. Of course, Gandalf knew the story of Sauron's Ring. He was starting to wonder what the cause of Bilbo's deceit could be and to connect it dimly with the Ring that had come so mysteriously into his possession.

IT'S A MISTAKE TO TALK DOWN TO CHILDREN

As Tolkien biographer Humphrey Carpenter notes, Tolkien changed his mind about how children should be addressed in a story.

For [*The Hobbit*] *is* a children's story. Despite the fact that it had been drawn into his mythology, Tolkien did not allow it to become overwhelmingly serious or even adult in tone, but stuck to his original intention of amusing his own and perhaps other people's children. Indeed he did this too consciously and deliberately at times in the first draft, which contains a large number of 'asides' to juvenile readers, remarks such as 'Now you know quite enough to go on with' and 'As we shall see in the end.' He later removed many of these, but some remain in the published text—to his regret, for he came to dislike them, and even to believe that any deliberate talking down to children is a great mistake in a story. 'Never mind about the young!' he once wrote. 'I am not interested in the "child" as such, modern or otherwise, and certainly have no intention of meeting him/her half way, or a quarter of the way. It is a mistaken thing to do anyway, either useless (when applied to the stupid) or pernicious (when inflicted on the gifted).' But when he wrote *The Hobbit* he was still suffering from what he later called 'the contemporary delusions about "fairy-stories" and children'—delusions that not long afterwards he made a conscious decision to renounce.

Humphrey Carpenter, *Tolkien: A Biography*. Boston: Houghton Mifflin, 1977.

By this new element prefacing *The Lord of the Rings*, as well as by some textual modifications in the later editions of *The Hobbit*, Tolkien provides for the necessary transition from the latter's mere ring of invisibility to the epic's great Ring of Power. Even so, of course, for the purpose of *The Hobbit* Bilbo's ring continues to be only a toy, useful for escapes and escapades, but having no deeper moral significance. No reader who had not previously read the epic would sense anything malefic about it. The story of *The Hobbit* has its own kind of logic quite different from that of the epic. To confuse them is to do a disservice to both tales. In sum, it is important to see *The Hobbit* as essentially independent of the epic, though serving as a quarry of important themes for the larger work. . . .

If *The Hobbit* is a quarry it is one in which the blocks of stone lie scattered about in a much looser and less imposing pattern than that in which the epic assembles those which it chooses to borrow. For example, Bilbo's enemies are serial, not united under any paragon of evil, as is to happen in the epic. *The Hobbit*'s trolls, goblins (orcs), spiders, and dragon know nothing of one another and are all acting on their own. They are certainly not shown to be servants of the nameless and nebulous Necromancer, whose only function in the story is to cause Gandalf to leave Bilbo and company to confront exciting perils unaided for a time. Nor, as has been said, is that magician linked in any way with the Ring, which comes out of nowhere belonging to no one. Also, as there is no alliance on behalf of evil so there is none against it. Dwarves, elves, and men act mainly for their selfish interests, often at cross-purposes, until a coalition is forced upon them by a goblin army hostile to all at the very end. Even then the issue is relatively localized and not worldwide in its ramifications. . . .

THE LEAP FROM CHILDREN'S TALE TO EPIC

The case is the same for the individual characters and the races in *The Hobbit* who will reappear in *The Lord of the Rings*. Tolkien's abrupt leap from a children's tale to an epic of heroic struggle requires a radical elevation of stature for all of them. . . .

Much of this need for upgrading the characters and the plot of *The Hobbit* arises from Tolkien's treatment of them in many situations of that tale as seriocomic. He evidently believes that the children will enjoy laughing at them some-

times, as a relief from shivering in excitement sympatheti-
cally with them at others. In truth, *The Hobbit* is seldom far
from comedy. Tolkien begins by making Bilbo the butt of
Gandalf's joke in sending the dwarves unexpectedly to eat up
all his food, proceeds on to the lamentable humor of the troll
scene, hangs his dwarves up in trees, rolls them in barrels,
touches the riddle scene with wit, makes the talk between
Bilbo and Smaug triumphantly ridiculous, and tops it all off
with Bilbo's return home to find his goods being auctioned
off and his reputation for respectable stupidity in ruins. It
must be acknowledged that the comedy is not invariably successful and that Tolkien's wry paternal manner of addressing
his young listeners does not always avoid an air of talking
down, which sets the teeth on edge. Nevertheless, *The Hobbit*
was never meant to be a wholly serious tale, nor his young
audience to listen without laughing often. In contradistinc-
tion, *The Lord of the Rings* does on occasion evoke smiles,
but most of the time its issues go too deep for laughter.

The Nature of Heroism in a Comic World

Katharyn F. Crabbe

Although Bilbo Baggins is a funny little character who seems to have little in common with the mythic, godlike heroes he admires, he is called to his own kind of heroism in *The Hobbit*, writes Katharyn F. Crabbe. He seems ridiculous in his first comic adventures, but gradually becomes the kind of hero Tolkien respects: the average person, without divine qualities, who is willing to risk his life for others. Besides the full-length study of Tolkien from which this essay is excerpted, Crabbe is the author of a biography of British author Evelyn Waugh.

Rather than being a simple and episodic little adventure story, *The Hobbit* is a carefully structured tale that uses a principle of progression (of journeys to the underworld, of the quality of opponents) to create a sense of working toward a climax. . . . The journey motif, the "There and Back Again" part of the story, encloses the two progressions in a circular structure which in turn gives the story a sense of completion.

Within the tidy circular structure, Tolkien develops two major and universal themes, both as accessible to children as they are to adults: the nature of heroism in a comic world and the conflict between good and evil. These are typical fairy-tale themes; however, Tolkien's fairy tale is distinguished from most others by the complexity he accords to these issues and by the way he combines them with a far less common theme in children's books, the power of language.

THE NATURE OF HEROISM

A distinctive part of Tolkien's fiction is his vision of what it means to be a hero and what is the nature of heroism. His

concern with heroism in *The Hobbit* is limited in scope to a
kind of hero we may call low mimetic—the hero who is no
better than we are, neither in kind nor in degree. And that
hero is, of course, Bilbo Baggins. From the first scenes of the
book, Bilbo's limitations, his differences from the high-
mimetic heroes of myth who are either gods or godlike men,
very different from us, are clear. Bilbo is "very respectable,"
which means he "never had any adventures or did anything
unexpected." Gandalf, the wizard, whose machinations set
Bilbo in motion, understands clearly that Bilbo is not a
mythic hero, and he understands that mythic heroes are
high mimetic, but as he points out to the dwarves, "I tried to
find one; but warriors are busy fighting one another in distant lands, and in this neighborhood heroes are scarce, or
simply not to be found." As in that most typical of British
fairy tales, "Jack the Giant Killer," the best possibility for
heroism in the Shire is to be found in a burglar.

Bilbo Baggins, then, has possibilities. He is, for example,
the son of "the fabulous Belladonna Took" and may through
her be descended from fairies. As a result, there is something more to Bilbo, "something that only [waits] for a
chance to come out." Furthermore, like many low-mimetic
heroes, Bilbo has a taste for real heroes of the high-mimetic
kind—he loves "wonderful tales . . . about dragons and goblins and giants and the rescue of princesses and the unexpected luck of widow's sons." That is, even the least likely
looking hobbit has by inheritance and imagination some
heroic possibilities.

HEROES AND NONHEROES

Just as Bilbo's sense of his own possibilities as a hero in-
creases throughout the story, so does the seriousness of his
motives. His first adventure, in which he and all the company
are captured by trolls, is strictly a comic event. Bilbo is de-
picted as a being of limited experience, one whose sheltered
life keeps him from understanding the ways of the world,
particularly the part of the world where people "have seldom
even heard of the King," that is, where the rules differ from
those of the Shire. Thus, his naivete, his lack of competence,
and his taste for animal comforts, which he shares with the
dwarves and the reader, are all roundly ridiculed.

As the book progresses, however, Bilbo's ridiculousness is
tempered with quite another quality. By the time he is cap-

tured and escapes from the goblins and from Gollum, his determination to return to the goblin caverns and search for his
friends has the effect of connecting him with two significant
high-mimetic heroes: Christ and Gandalf. The connection
with Christ is tenuous but real, resulting from the conjunction of the language of the passage with the New Testament
"greater love hath no man than this: that he lay down his life
for his friend," as Tolkien writes, "He wondered whether he
ought not, now he had the magic ring, to go back into the
horrible, horrible tunnels and look for his friends." The connection with Gandalf is less tenuous; it results from Bilbo's
willingness to assume the role of shepherd that Gandalf has
portrayed so far and is trying to persuade the dwarves to help
him portray again: "Gandalf was saying that they could not
possibly go on with their journey leaving Mr. Baggins in the
hands of the goblins without trying to find out if he was alive
or dead, and without trying to rescue him."

"After all he is my friend," said the wizard, "and not a bad
little chap." Gandalf and Bilbo, the high-mimetic and low-
mimetic heroes, sharing a willingness to return to the "horrible, horrible tunnels" to save their friends, are set apart
from the dwarves, who are ruled by their own fears: "If we
have got to go back now into those abominable tunnels to
look for him, then drat him, I say." Dwarves are not, as the
narrator says later, bad people, but they are not heroes.

Influences Beyond the Hero's Control

Once Bilbo and Gandalf are set up as representing the low-
mimetic and high-mimetic sides of the hero, Gandalf may
leave to attend to "some pressing business away south." His
concern with and responsibility for the world beyond, fore-
shadowed early in his meeting Thorin's father in the dungeons of the Necromancer and in his decision not to let the
Wargs "have it all their own way," looks forward to his return in time for the Battle of the Five Armies with its wider
implications for Middle-earth.

Gandalf leaves Thorin and Company with a series of
warnings that sound very like Christian's exhortations to
himself in *Pilgrim's Progress:* "We may meet again before
this is all over and then again we may not. That depends on
your luck and on your courage and sense." That is, not
everything is foreordained. Both God and man have a hand
in shaping all that happens: God through the medium of

grace, which Tolkien calls "luck," and man through his physical and rational excellences, bravery and sense, which, at their best, represent the God-like in man.

That Gandalf is only a hero of a higher order or perhaps a messenger of God is suggested by his own limitations—he can be afraid, though he is a wizard and, he admits, his success in bringing the troop through the mountains has depended upon the same forces on which they must rely— "good management and good luck."

THE LONER AND THE SOCIAL HERO

While Gandalf, the high-mimetic hero, is a loner, one particularly important quality in Bilbo's heroism as it develops in the episodes before Thorin and Company reach the city of Esgaroth upon the long lake is its essential socialness. From the moment Bilbo bursts out of his house without his pipe or his pipe-weed, or even a pocket-handkerchief, his movement has always been *toward* the dwarves. Separated from them by Wood-elves, he always moves toward the company of the adventurers. The paradox is that although he always moves *toward*, Bilbo is also always gaining in confidence, competence, and character—all the qualities that lead to self-sufficiency. By the time the dwarves escape from the caverns of the Wood-elves, Bilbo is clearly the leader, and even Thorin must agree to follow him. In doing what he must do to remain a part of the group, Bilbo takes responsibility for it; taking responsibility makes him a leader and sets him apart, isolates him from the group, as illustrated in the description of the escape from the caverns of the Wood-elves: "He was in the dark tunnel, floating in icy water, all alone—for you cannot count friends that are all packed up in barrels."

A WIDER RESPONSIBILITY

By the time of the escape from the Wood-elves, Bilbo has developed as far as is possible in the direction of his small society. Yet the end of the quest has not been achieved. The possibilities for continuing are two: Bilbo may stop in his development (as Mark Twain's Tom Sawyer does) and simply lead the dwarves to the treasure, or he may continue to develop in some way that parallels the continuation of the quest. The first possibility is unlikely, for it would reduce the importance of the final episode to a simple working out of plot. The tale would become mere episodic adventure instead of a unified quest. But if Bilbo is to continue to develop, which direction must he take? The answer is provided in Gandalf's example: As Gandalf's "some pressing business away south" suggests a responsibility to the wider world beyond the company, Bilbo eventually finds that he has a wider responsibility, too—to the men of Esgaroth, to the king of the Wood-elves, to the Five Armies. And yet, Thorin and Company cannot be utterly deserted, for they are a part of that wider world too.

The movement of Bilbo away from the society of Thorin and Company is evident as soon as the party leaves Esgaroth for the Lonely Mountain—and it is here that the sense of making Bilbo a hobbit rather than another dwarf or an elf becomes clear—he is with the company but not of them. Though the company finds the door in the mountain without too much delay, they are quite unable to guess its secret until a day when "the dwarves all went wandering off in various directions. . . . All day Bilbo sat gloomily in the grassy bay gazing at the stone, or out west through the narrow opening." Here the real movement of Bilbo away from the company begins, and it begins in contemplation of the west—the source of wisdom and creativity, though also the symbol of the end.

THE HERO INITIATES ACTION

Tolkien uses structural repetition to demonstrate Bilbo's growth in this episode. Once the door is opened and Bilbo is in the tunnel, the situation is very like that following the escape from the goblins' tunnel when Bilbo was pursued by Gollum: He accepts his duty to do for the dwarves, even though he cannot (and does not) hope that the dwarves will do for him:

> The most that can be said for the dwarves is this: they intended to pay Bilbo really handsomely for his services; they had brought him to do a nasty job for them, and they did not mind the little fellow doing it if he would; but they would all have done their best to get him out of trouble, if he got into it, as they did in the case of the trolls at the beginning of their adventures before they had any reason for being grateful to him. There it is: dwarves are not heroes, but calculating folk with a great idea of the value of money; some are tricky and treacherous and pretty bad lots; some are not, but are decent enough people like Thorin and Company, if you don't expect too much.

There are two important suggestions about Tolkien's view of the nature of heroism in this passage. First, it suggests that heroism is active rather than reactive, because Thorin and Company are steady and brave in rescuing friends in need, as Thorin's reaction when Smaug leaves his den will show. But Bilbo must be the initiator of action, not just a reactor. And he becomes an initiator when he steps into the tunnel and begins, for the first time, to move out away from the company and toward the wide world. As was true when he escaped from the goblins, his most heroic act in this scene is a psychological one: Once out of the horrible goblin caves, Bilbo had decided to go back inside to search for his companions if necessary. Here, once inside the tunnel, Bilbo makes another heroic decision—to keep going further despite the agonizing fear he feels when he hears Smaug's snoring and sees his red glow.

This is an important step for Bilbo, because it transforms him. Smaug's dream, prophetic as it is, features no burglars and no grocers. Instead, it is "an uneasy dream (in which a warrior, altogether insignificant in size, but provided with a bitter sword and great courage, figured most unpleasantly)." In deciding to go on alone, Bilbo becomes the warrior that Gandalf was looking for, and Smaug's dream of a warrior foreshadows the gift of the mithril mail Thorin will give Bilbo in recognition of his bravery.

THE HERO CONTINUES WHEN HOPE IS GONE

In the encounter with Smaug, the confrontation with the men of Dale, and the Battle of the Five Armies, Bilbo demonstrates the final defining quality of his low-mimetic heroism, the ability to go on when there is no hope. Whether the issue is recovering the treasure by getting rid of Smaug ("Personally, I have no hopes at all . . ."), or rescuing dwarves from Wood-elves ("he was not as hopeful as they were"), Bilbo's hopelessness is always short-lived and gives way to hope that springs from plans and action. Though Bilbo's states of hopelessness never last as long as Frodo's will in *The Lord of the Rings*, Tolkien sounds the first notes of the theme in *The Hobbit*.

By the closing chapters of the story, the reader has long understood that Bilbo's capacity for physical bravery is far greater than he thought, so we are not surprised when, in the Battle of the Five Armies, he draws his sword to stand with the Elvenking. But the side of heroism Bilbo reveals in giving up the Arkenstone, the sacrificial act that repudiates the heart of the mountain and the heart of Thorin, is a binding force: It draws men to it and binds them. Bilbo's giving up the arkenstone, that is, his expressing a commitment to the wider world that comes before his commitment to Thorin and Company, unites him not only with Gandalf but also with the high-mimetic hero, Bard.

BEINGS OF HEROIC PROPORTION VS. ORDINARY HEROES

Bard, as the high-mimetic hero Bilbo is not, foreshadows the kind of heroism that will be represented by Aragorn, the king of men, in *The Lord of the Rings*. He is a man of heroic stature, the descendant of kings, and the protector of his people. Thus he is the kind of hero who may be expected to slay dragons, a traditional high-mimetic heroic feat. Furthermore, like Aragorn, Bard is a healer. After Smaug's destruction of Esgaroth, he is quick "to help in the ordering of the camps and in the care of the sick and the wounded," and when he approaches Thorin to demand a portion of the treasure, he asks for it in the name of justice, but also in the name of mercy.

High-mimetic heroism, then, of the kind demonstrated by warrior kings and other men or demigods of heroic proportions appears in *The Hobbit* not so much as a vision of heroism in which Tolkien is particularly interested at this time, but as a background against which the quality of Bilbo's heroism (and by implication, the heroism of which the reader is capable) may be more clearly seen. The viewing of Bilbo's deeds against the assumptions about heroes underlying the heroism of Gandalf and Bard illustrates clearly that the ordinary man, though he cannot work magic or kill dragons, can do what a hero does: He can save us. It also illustrates that the qualities of the low-mimetic hero need not be great strength or great wisdom, but a kind heart, a hopeful disposition, and a love of his fellow beings. As Gandalf reminds Bilbo at the end of the story, "You are a very fine person, Mr. Baggins, and I am fond of you; but you are only quite a little fellow in a wide world after all." Indeed, suggests Tolkien, so are we all.

Psychological Themes in *The Hobbit*

Dorothy Matthews

Although its resemblance to certain nursery tales
may keep it from being taken seriously, *The Hobbit*
provides some profound insights into the human
psyche, writes Dorothy Matthews. Exploring the un-
balanced masculine and feminine sides of Bilbo Baggins's personality, Matthews traces the steps he takes
to bring the two sides of his character into harmony.
Matthews chaired the National Council of Teachers
of English Committee to revise NCTE's annotated list
of High Interest–Easy Reading books for high school
and junior high school students.

Since its publication in 1938, J.R.R. Tolkien's *The Hobbit* has
received very little serious critical attention other than as the
precursor of *The Lord of the Rings*. It has usually been
praised as a good introduction to the trilogy, and as a children's book, but anyone familiar with psychoanalysis cannot
avoid being tantalized by recurrent themes and motifs. . . . Bilbo's story has surprising depths that can be
plumbed by the reader who is receptive to psychoanalytic
interpretations.

The central pattern of *The Hobbit* is, quite obviously, a quest.
Like so many heroes before him, Bilbo sets out on a perilous
journey, encounters and overcomes many obstacles (including
a confrontation with a dragon) and returns victorious after he
has restored a kingdom and righted ancient wrongs. However,
this pattern is so commonplace in literature that it is not a very
helpful signpost. But it may help in other ways.

Let us first look briefly at *The Hobbit* for its folk ingredi-
ents, that is, the common motifs or story elements which it
shares with folk narratives. There are, of course, the crea-

tures themselves: dwarves, elves, trolls, animal servants, helpful birds and, the most frequently recurring of all folk adversaries, the treasure-guarding dragon. There are magic objects in abundance: a ring of invisibility, secret entrances into the underworld, magic swords, and doors into mountains. Dreams foretell and taboos admonish, the violation of which could bring dire results.

There are tasks to be performed, riddles to solve, and foes to be outwitted or outfought. Folk motifs form the very warp and woof in the texture of this tale, which is not surprising since Tolkien, as a medievalist, is immersed in folk tradition, a tradition that gives substance not only to the best known epics but to most medieval narratives and to "fairy tales."

In fact, it is probably its resemblance to what today's readers see as the nursery tale that has resulted in *The Hobbit* being relegated to elementary school shelves. The fat, comfort-loving Bilbo can easily remind a reader of Winnie-the-Pooh, who had to have his "little something" at eleven o'clock or of another epicurean, Peter Rabbit, who risked all for a feast in Farmer McGregor's garden. Bilbo's home-loving nature can also call to mind the domestic Water Rat and Mole of Kenneth Grahame's *Wind in the Willows*, for Bilbo found the sound of a kettle singing out to announce the hour for tea the most heartening in the world. And Bilbo's descent into the depths of the mountain where he loses track of time and finds himself confronted by menacing and riddling adversaries certainly bears a resemblance to *Alice's Adventures in Wonderland*. Bilbo also can be seen as similar to such diminutive heroes of international fairy tales as the master of "Puss-in-Boots," "Jack in the Beanstalk," and the endless stream of youngest of three sons who, through no outstanding qualities of their own, are propelled to riches and renown through the aid of magic objects or supernatural helpers.

INSIGHTS INTO THE HUMAN PSYCHE

But even if *The Hobbit* is only a children's story, it should be analyzed more closely for deeper levels of meaning, for it is the kind of story that has provided the most profound insights into the human psyche.

Both Freud's and Jung's studies of folk materials supported the theory that the unconscious expresses itself through such channels as dreams and fantasy. The protagonist in so many of these tales encounters his greatest obstacles alone, as a dreamer. Even in large-scale epics the hero fights single-handedly although the stakes are much higher than in fairy tales. Beowulf confronts both Grendel and Grendel's mother alone, and [King] Arthur and Modred, as the only survivors on a corpse-strewn battlefield, decide the future of the kingdom through man-to-man struggle. It is also suggestive that the descents in so many of these stories have a universal appeal. Trips into the underworld abound in Greek hero tales and myths as well as in Germanic lore. Just as Orpheus seeks Eurydice, just as Beowulf goes down into the sea to fight Grendel's mother in her lair, just as Alice falls into an underground realm, so Bilbo descends into the heart of the mountain to encounter Gollum and, later, Smaug. Freudian symbolism might also explain the prominence given in well-known tales to the nicknames of swords such as *The Hobbit*'s Orcrist (the Biter) and Glamdring the Foe-Hammer (the Beater), the acquisition of which is an important event in the life of the hero. Some of the most memorable episodes in the Arthurian tales are those describing Arthur's passing the test devised to identify the rightful king by miraculously freeing the sword from the stone, and his receiving the gem-encrusted Excalibur from the lady of the Lake. If Freud's view of the sword as a phallic symbol is correct, then it does not seem farfetched to view these scenes as vestiges of the coming-into-manhood ritual. Surely Freudian sex symbols are found with startling frequency in these stories. Recall, for instance, the prominence of keys, locks, caves, chalices, and cups in these works. . . .

BILBO'S POTENTIAL

When we are first introduced to Bilbo, he is far from being a boy hobbit in terms of years, but his maturity is questionable. His primary concerns, like those of any child, are with physical comforts. Eating is probably his favorite activity. He seldom ventures from his hobbit hole, a dwelling interestingly womblike in its isolation from the shocks of the world. Bilbo is noticeably annoyed when Gandalf arrives with the dwarf visitors since he would prefer to live what appears to be a somewhat withdrawn, self-centered life.

Early in the story it is clear, however, that Bilbo has much more in him than he is giving expression to. The potential for tension lies between the Baggins and the Took sides of his nature; through his mother, Belladonna Took, he is related to an adventurous family and has inherited aggressive tendencies. However, he has evidently repressed this more spirited side of his personality in favor of the Baggins impulses, which tend to be rather fuddy-duddy and more than a little feminine. Bilbo is much more interested, for instance, in keeping a tidy house, cooking a tempting meal, and keeping himself in pocket handkerchiefs than he is in venturing boldly into the world to find what life may have in store for him.

In other words, at the beginning of the tale, Bilbo's personality is out of balance and far from integrated. His masculinity, or one may say his Tookish aggressiveness, is being repressed so that he is clinging rather immaturely to a childish way of life. He has not even begun to realize his full potential. The womblike peace and security of his home is disturbed with the arrival of Gandalf, who may be seen as a projection of the Jungian archetype of the "wise old man" since he resembles the magic helper of countless stories: Merlin of the Arthurian cycle, Odin of Norse legend, or the helpful old person of the fairy tale, to name but a few. Like his prototypes, Gandalf sounds the call to adventure and motivates the reluctant hobbit to leave his home, helps him in the early stages of his venture into perilous realms, and then leaves him when he can stand alone.

At the outset of their adventure, Bilbo, like a typical young adolescent, is uncertain of his role, or "persona," to use a Jungian term. The dwarves quickly reinforce his insecurity; Gandalf asked him to join the group to be a burglar, but the dwarves carp that he acts more like a grocer than a burglar.

He fears that he cannot live up to Gandalf's expectations, and during the early conflicts with the trolls and goblins, Bilbo is completely dependent upon the wizard for help. The most prominent force in these early events is luck, or chance. It is only through chance that the key to the trolls' cave is found, thus providing unearned access to the magic swords so necessary for later trials. If the sword is seen as a phallic symbol, its miraculous appearance at the beginning of the journey supports the ritualistic pattern of maturation in Bilbo's adventures.

THE DECISION TO FACE LIFE

One of the most crucial incidents of the story takes place when Bilbo finds himself unconscious and separated from the dwarves within the mountain domain of the goblins. In this underground scene he must face an important trial; he must make a decision whose outcome will be a measure of his maturity. After accidentally finding the ring, Bilbo wonders whether or not he should summon up the courage to face whatever dangers await him. Unlike the unsure, regressive hobbit he was, Bilbo suddenly exclaims: "Go Back? No good at all! Go sideways? Impossible! Go Forward? Only thing to do!" For the first time Bilbo finds within himself a strength he didn't know he possessed. With unprecedented courage he decides to face life rather than to withdraw from it. This decision marks an important step in his psychological journey.

The danger he decides to face at this time, of course, is Gollum, the vaguely sensed but monstrous inhabitant of the underground lake. The association of this adversary with water and the attention given to his long grasping fingers and voracious appetite suggest a similarity to Jung's Devouring-Mother archetype, that predatory monster which must be faced and slain by every individual in the depths of his unconscious if he is to develop as a self-reliant individual. The fact that the talisman is a ring is even more suggestive of Jungian symbology since the circle is a Jungian archetype of the *self*—the indicator of possible psychic wholeness. The psychological importance of this confrontation is further supported by the imagery of the womb and of rebirth which marks the details of Bilbo's escape.

Wearing the ring of invisibility, Bilbo finally makes his way to the exit from the subterranean realm of darkness only to find a menacing figure humped against the opening. The gleaming, cold green eyes tell him it is Gollum.

> Bilbo almost stopped breathing, and went stiff himself. He was desperate. He must get away, out of this horrible darkness, while he had any strength left. He must fight. . . . And he was miserable, alone, lost . . . thoughts passed in a flash of a second. He trembled. And then quite suddenly in another flash, as if lifted by a new strength and resolve, he leaped . . . a leap in the dark . . . he only missed cracking his skull on the low arch of the passage.

Narrowly missed by Gollum's desperate effort to grab him, Bilbo begins falling and lands in a new tunnel. The text continues:

> Soon the passage that had been sloping down began to go up again, and after a while it climbed steeply. That slowed Bilbo down. But at last the slope stopped, the passage turned a corner and dipped down again, and there at the bottom of a short incline, he saw, filtering round another corner—a glimpse of light. Not red light, as of fire or lantern, but a pale out-of-doors sort of light.

REBIRTH

But Bilbo is no sooner out of the reach of Gollum when he is confronted by new dangers from the goblins. Here again the ring helps him in his escape, which is described in terms highly suggestive of the traumatic natal experience:

> "I must get to the door, I must get to the door!" he kept saying to himself, but it was a long time before he ventured to try. Then it was like a horrible game of blindman's bluff. The place was full of goblins running about, and the poor little hobbit dodged this way and that, was knocked over by a goblin who could not make out what he had bumped into, scrambled away on all fours, slipped between the legs of the captain just in time, got up and ran for the door.
>
> It was still ajar.... Bilbo struggled but he could not move it. He tried to squeeze through the crack. He squeezed and squeezed, and he stuck! It was awful.... He could see outside into the open air: ... but he could not get through....
>
> Bilbo's heart jumped into his mouth. He gave a terrific squirm. Buttons burst off in all directions. He was through.

The suggestion of rebirth symbolically expressed in these passages is consistently carried out in the episodes that follow, and they clearly demonstrate that a metamorphosis has indeed taken place. When Bilbo rejoins his friends, he is unquestionably changed. The dwarves begin to notice a difference when, through the aid of his ring, Bilbo is able to appear suddenly in their midst without detection, a feat much more befitting a burglar than a grocer. The delight and astonishment experienced by the dwarves is felt even more deeply by Gandalf, who is "probably more pleased than all the others."

> It is a fact that Bilbo's reputation went up a very great deal with the dwarves after this. If they had still doubted that he was really a first-class burglar, in spite of Gandalf's words, they doubted no longer.

The new respect which Bilbo has earned from his companions in turn leads to increased self-confidence; he is becoming a very different kind of hobbit. His decision to face danger has profoundly changed him.

STABILIZING THE NEWLY BALANCED PERSONALITY

The Tookish and Baggins sides of his personality have been brought into a new harmony. His Baggins impulses are beginning to be counter-balanced, thus bringing about a desirable psychic tension, which can result only when a balance of opposites exists. This is not the end of the journey, however, for the sudden change must be stabilized through reinforcing experiences. In fact, Gandalf remains with the party to see them through the adventure with the wargs and the goblins. It is during this episode that Gandalf summons help from the eagles, an act with possible symbolic significance since, according to Jung, the bird archetype is a powerful transforming agent. Similarly Beorn, with his interesting man-beast metamorphic possibilities, fits surprisingly well into Jung's conjectures regarding the archetypal figures of the unconscious.

The topography of the journey also has possible metaphoric significance. It is within a mountain reached through an underground descent that Bilbo finds the ring and passes his first trial. It is now within a wood, Mirkwood, that Gandalf puts Bilbo in charge of the group. Woods have long been recognized as an archetype for danger, so Mirkwood is the appropriate setting for Bilbo to demonstrate his self-reliance. The wizard leaves his charge alone at the edge of the forest to face this next important test of manhood in the woods, and the spider finds Bilbo worthy of Gandalf's trust. He not only finds the courage to confront his adversary; he actually distinguishes himself by his valor. The monstrous enemy that threatens to hold and enmesh the hero in its web is a common metaphor for the paralysis of the victim, symbolically in a state of psychic fixation.

Whether the spider with whom Bilbo battles is interpreted as a Jungian shadow figure, embodying evil, or as the Devouring-Mother facet of the anima is immaterial. The symbolism is clear without specific terms: a lone protagonist must free himself from a menacing opponent that has the power to cripple him forever. With the aid of a miraculously acquired sword and a magic talisman, he is able to face the danger and overcome it. . . .

From this point on, Bilbo has the self-esteem needed to fulfill his responsibilities as a mature and trustworthy leader. It is through his ingenuity that they escape from the dungeon prisons in the subterranean halls of the wood-elves. This last episode also reveals telling symbolic details in that the imprisonment is underground and the escape through a narrow outlet into the water is yet another birth image.

FINAL STAGES OF THE QUEST OF MATURATION

The climactic adventures of Bilbo are of course the episodes with Smaug, who, like the traditional dragon of folklore, has

laid waste the land and is guarding a treasure. If viewed in
the light of Jungian symbology, the contested treasure can
be seen as the archetype of the self, of psychic wholeness.
Thus this last series of events marks the final stages of
Bilbo's quest of maturation.

When the group arrives at the Lonely Mountain (another
site aptly symbolic), it is noteworthy that it is Bilbo who
prods the dwarves into beginning the dangerous search for
the secret door. The helpful bird motif is again instrumental;
this time, in accordance with the message read by Elrond
from the moon letters on the map, the tapping of a thrush
alerts Bilbo to look for the keyhole which is suddenly visible
in the rays of the setting sun. The discovery of the door,
swinging open with the turn of the key, presents the hobbit
with his greatest challenge so far. Knowing that the dwarves
expect him to be the one to explore the secret passage, Bilbo
is ready with a response, even before he is asked:

> . . . I have got you out of two messes already, which were hardly
> in the original bargain, so that I am, I think, already owed some
> reward. But third time pays for all as my father used to say, and
> somehow I don't think I shall refuse. Perhaps I have begun to
> trust my luck more than I used to in the old days.

Although his request for company on this dangerous mis-
sion is turned down, Bilbo nonetheless courageously enters
through the enchanted door, steals into the mountain, puts
on his ring, and creeps noiselessly "down, down, down into
the dark. He was trembling with fear, but his little face was
set and grim. Already he was a very different hobbit from the
one that had run out without a pocket-handkerchief from
Bag-End long ago. He had not had a pocket-handkerchief for
ages. He loosened his dagger in its sheath, tightened his belt,
and went on."

And so with this description, Tolkien makes it clear that
Bilbo is facing his most demanding trial of physical courage
by daring to descend alone into the dragon's lair. With every
step, Bilbo feels internal conflict:

> "Now you are in for it at last, Bilbo Baggins," he said to him-
> self. "You went and put your foot right in it that night of the
> party, and now you have got to pull it out and pay for it! Dear
> me, what a fool I was and am!" said the least Tookish part of
> him. "I have absolutely no use for dragon-guarded treasures,
> and the whole lot could stay here forever, if only I would
> wake up and find this beastly tunnel was my own front-hall
> at home."

If he is ever to turn back, the time for it comes when his senses are assailed by the heat, the red light burning even brighter, and the terrifying sounds of bubbling and rumbling coming from the dragon hole. Tolkien describes this climactic moment:

> It was at this point that Bilbo stopped. Going on from there was the bravest thing he ever did. The tremendous things that happened afterwards were as nothing compared to it. He fought the real battle in the tunnel alone, before he ever saw the vast danger that lay in wait.

From this point on, Bilbo's physical courage is unquestioned. It is true that his reputation flags a little when his first descent into the dragon's den touches off a devastating rampage, but he reasserts his leadership during the second descent by learning of the dragon's one vulnerable spot, the piece of information so vital in finally ridding the land of its menace. In the last descent Bilbo acquires the Arkenstone, the gem so important to both the elves and the dwarves. Again, it is significant to note that the incident incorporates Jungian symbols, for the problem presented by the Arkenstone results in a different kind of test for Bilbo. To solve it he needs moral rather than physical courage.

BILBO AS ANTI-HERO

A truly critical question arises in considering this incident and the remainder of the story. I have taught this work many times and am constantly hearing complaints of dissatisfaction from students who feel that the last part of the book is both puzzling and anticlimactic. Many report that they felt a real loss of interest while reading the final chapters. Why does Bilbo keep the Arkenstone without telling the dwarves and then use it as a pawn in dealing with their enemies? Why, they ask, did Tolkien have a rather uninteresting character, rather than Bilbo, kill Smaug? Why is Bilbo, the previous center of interest, knocked unconscious so that he is useless during the last Battle of Five Armies? Isn't it a fault in artistic structure to allow the protagonist to fade from the picture during episodes when the normal expectation would be to have him demonstrate even more impressive heroism?

Answers to these questions are clear if the story is interpreted as the psychological journey of Bilbo Baggins. It stands to reason that Tolkien does not have Bilbo kill the dragon because that would be more the deed of a savior or culture hero, such as St. George, or the Red Cross Knight, or Beowulf. The significance of this tale lies in fact in the very obviously anti-heroic manner in which Tolkien chooses to bring Bilbo's adventures to a conclusion. As a result, Bilbo emerges as a symbol of a very average individual, not as a figure of epic proportions. Bilbo has not found eternal glory, but, rather, the self-knowledge that a willingness to meet challenge is not necessarily incompatible with a love of home. By giving expression to his Tookishness, he has found a new harmony and balance. And in realizing his full potential, Bilbo demonstrates that even his Baggins side provides him with values that are not without importance. Thorin recognizes this special worth in his final tribute to the hobbit:

> There is more in you of good than you know, child of the friendly west. Some courage and some wisdom, blended in measure. If more of us valued food and cheer and song above hoarded gold, it would be a merrier world.

Thus, at the conclusion of his adventures Bilbo finds the greatest prize of all: a knowledge of his own identity. In maturing psychologically, he has learned to think for himself and to have the courage to follow a course he knows to be right—in spite of possible repercussions. This maturity is demonstrated in the Arkenstone episode. His decision to use the gem as a means of negotiating with the opposition is made with the knowledge that it might mean the sacrifice of his friendship with Thorin and the dwarves. But Bilbo makes that choice. Like the hero in a medieval romance, he is confronted with a dilemma. Like Gawain, he has to face moral as well as physical trials. Bilbo makes the decision independently, trusting his own judgment and being willing to face censure and, if necessary, isolation. Bilbo's solution to his ethical problem satisfied Gandalf. The initiate has survived all ordeals successfully. In achieving self-reliance and self-knowledge, he had indeed found the Jungian jewel hard to attain. And furthermore, Bilbo knows the role he was created to fill, for when Gandalf tells him: "You're a very fine person . . . but you are only a little fellow in a wide world, after all," the hobbit answers simply, "Thank goodness."

A Jungian Interpretation

Timothy R. O'Neill

Timothy R. O'Neill is the author of *The Individuated Hobbit: Jung, Tolkien, and the Archetypes of Middle-earth*, from which this viewpoint is excerpted. In it, O'Neill relates Carl Jung's psychology of self-realization to Bilbo's growth throughout *The Hobbit*. Ego, shadow, libido, the unconscious—all are given potent images in this tale of the hobbit who refuses treasures of wealth in favor of the treasure of the Self.

Bilbo Baggins of Bag End was as conventional a hobbit as any other—despite the influence of his scandalous mother—and, like his conservative associates, eschewed adventure in all its distasteful forms. The most dangerous adventure of all, of course, is the journey into one's own psyche; and it is just that adventure that Bilbo undertakes in the fiftieth year of his life.

Nor is he really dragged kicking and screaming by the wizard and thirteen Dwarves. As they sang of the silence and majesty, the gleaming crystal columns and torchlit halls of the Lonely Mountain, Bilbo felt a stirring in his heart:

> Then something Tookish woke up inside him, and he wished to go and see the great mountains, and hear the pine-trees and the waterfalls, and explore the caves, and wear a sword instead of a walking stick.[1]

But this glimpse of the shadow world, the sudden revealing of a forgotten strain of Tookishness, is too much for this watchful, timid hobbit consciousness:

> Suddenly in the wood beyond The Water a flame leapt up— probably somebody lighting a wood fire—and he thought of plundering dragons settling on his quiet Hill and kindling it all to flames. He shuddered; and very quickly he was plain Mr. Baggins of Bag End, Under-Hill, again.[2]

1. J.R.R. Tolkien, *The Hobbit* (New York: Ballantine Books, 1966), p. 28. 2. Ibid.

Excerpted from *The Individuated Hobbit: Jung, Tolkien, and the Archetypes of Middle-earth*, by Timothy R. O'Neill. Copyright © 1979 by Timothy R. O'Neill. Reprinted by permission of Houghton Mifflin Company. All rights reserved.

The potency of these newly awakened symbols is so compelling that Bilbo must suppress the strange and disquieting feelings they evoke, unbidden, from the depths of what serves a hobbit for an unconscious. The Tookishness subsides.

This "Tookishness" is explicitly personified as the "fabulous Belladonna Took," Bilbo's mother. It is a female figure; a magical, potent figure out of Faërie, and the author and manipulator of his urges to climb above his humdrum hobbit existence. It is also his link with the collective past—the narrator speculates that some hobbit in the Took genealogy must have taken a fairy (Elvish) wife, another reference to the mystical and reverential, dimensions quite foreign to hobbit affairs. This is the first inkling that Bilbo is about to break out of his one-sided life, and it frightens him. Well it might, for even in the brave departure from the Shire, "running as fast as his furry feet could carry him,"[3] he could not have guessed what horrors lay ahead. How many hobbits of his generation had been obliged to deal with trolls, or seen trolls, or even believed in them? Only Bilbo, one presumes.

A WORLD OF SYMBOLS

And fearsome trolls they are. Bilbo's world is a dream world, a Faërie world; and in the world of dreams, of the psyche, the aggressive animal may symbolize unrestrained libido.[4] The trolls, although nominally anthropomorphic, seem to fall into this functional category—if there was ever inarticulate, unrestrained libido in action, it is the trio of Bert, Bill, and Tom. This may be regarded as the first sign of the power, the numinous potency, of the complexes that reside in Bilbo's unconscious. . . .

The travelers' brief respite in Rivendell allows the interpretation of Thorin's map, and the secrets hidden in it by magic are revealed by Elrond. Elrond is a symbol of the union of opposites (Elf and Man); it is only logical that he should be the one to find the key to the map—the moon-letters, runes that are revealed only by moonlight. He brings forth the hidden instructions ("stand by the grey stone when the thrush knocks") from the depths of the unconscious, the clue which will unlock the secrets of the hidden psyche. The moon is often connected, at least in the male psyche, with

3. Ibid., p. 41. 4. Carl G. Jung, *The Collected Works of Carl G. Jung*, vol. 5, *Symbols of Transformation* (New York: Pantheon, 1967), p. 328.

the unconscious, as the sun may symbolize in men's dreams and imagination the conscious.

After their departure from Rivendell, wizard, Dwarves, and hobbit are confronted by a mountain storm; the sudden fury and flashes of lightning portend symbolically the approach of a sudden psychic change, and the change which is about to occur is the most dramatic and significant of all.

Bilbo's progress thus far has only hinted at the coming crisis, the first stirrings of a change that may express the symptoms of neurosis; but this is not the real psyche, only a dream psyche. The appearance of certain portents, numinous images charged with inflated power that surge from the depths of the unconscious, serve as warnings—warnings that invariably make Bilbo long for the solid comfort of his hobbit-hole. The last thing Mr. Baggins wants to undertake at this point is a journey Under Hill into the depths of his forgotten mind and a confrontation with the unlovely demons of the imagination that lurk there. Attention is reversed now, from an outward to an inward perspective, and the frightful fiend is thus ahead rather than behind. But with thirteen Dwarves pulling him on and a wizard standing rear guard to head off any thoughts of malingering, Bilbo must march on.

Descent may symbolize the direction of attention and energy into the unconscious, and this is where Bilbo is dumped unceremoniously during the party's headlong flight from the pursuing mountain goblins. Lost and alone, he stumbles exhausted, and his hand finds—by chance?—the Ring. . . .

DESCENT INTO THE UNCONSCIOUS

"Deep down here by the dark water lived old Gollum, a small slimy creature."[5]. . . Gollum paddles about his little cold pool of water deep at the mountain's roots. The deep water is associated symbolically with the unconscious, with depth and knowledge and wisdom. Bilbo's progress has thus been *descent* into the *unconscious*, in the first timid search for enlightenment. But true wisdom for Bilbo must be shunted aside—the first order of business is to get out of that mountain as soon as possible. The revelations of the unconscious are really too much! The key to escape is slimy old Gollum, repulsive though he may be. Their riddle game is a

5. Tolkien, *The Hobbit*, p. 79.

duel of conscious and unconscious preoccupations. Bilbo
marshals images of an egg (symbolizing the eye of the conscious), eating (material world), sun on the daisies (*sol* as
representation of the conscious); Gollum relies upon contrasting pictures: wind, darkness, the roots of mountains,
fish. But Bilbo is careless and fated to be anything but rid of
Gollum, whatever the outcome of the riddle game. He gives
Gollum his *name*—an important piece of information not to
be blurted heedlessly to anyone, much less a mildewy
green-eyed figure of shadow who lives in a cave, eats raw
goblins caught unawares, and talks to himself. And Bilbo,
above all, has the Ring, in whose shining symmetry is en-
cased Gollum's dark soul. . . .

EGO AND SHADOW

Bilbo is clearly the ego, as the focal personality thus far in
the story. More than this, Bilbo is the reader's ego. Bilbo's adventure has become the reader's dream, his creative, vicari-
ous inner experience. The ego has courageously (more or
less) entered the forbidden recesses of the unconscious and
collided unexpectedly with its dark mirror image. The colli-
sion is brief and incomplete—the two are now for the first
time fully aware of each other's existence, and their fates are
inseparably bound. The only possible end of this dream lies
many years and many miles ahead, at the Cracks of Doom.

Ego and shadow face each other at the twilit border of
dark and light, and they are tied together by a precious ring,
the One Ring, the "One Ring to find them/One Ring to bring
them all and in the darkness bind them." This is the ruling
Ring, for it rules both their fates; and these fates are bound,
as is foretold, "in the Land of Mordor where the Shadows
lie."[6] . . .

The Ring is the focal point of the *symbolic* story, and as
such subtly overwhelms the overt plot like the latent content
of a dream that belies the manifest experience. To say that
either *The Hobbit* or *The Lord of the Rings* is a tale of there
and back again is to suggest that [Dante's] *Divine Comedy* is
a book about cave exploring. Tolkien's faërie world is a
world of light and dark, a realm with very few softer tones
(and whenever a character seems to assume a mantle of
grey ambivalence, the cause is invariably the Ring). At the

6. J.R.R. Tolkien, *The Lord of the Rings* (New York: Ballantine Books, 1970), I:81.

border is the twilight, the furthest marches of the conscious, where things are not as they seem; and binding these realms together is the precious Ring.

The Ring is perfect in form, and stands for the Self. . . . The Ring's symmetry is perfectly balanced, a graceful circle, distilling the concepts of balance and perfection and the union of all opposites that will characterize the Self after its realization. Its material is gold, because of its incorruptible nature as in the philosophy of alchemy. Jung was fascinated by the complex and powerful imagery of medieval alchemy. . . . In any case, the form and function of the Ring are not left in doubt. The Ring's fate is etched inside and out in fiery letters:

> *One Ring to rule them all, One Ring to find them.*
> *One Ring to bring them all and in the darkness bind them.*[7]

The Ring is the Self, the potential force that promises finally to make whole both hobbit and Middle-earth.

But Bilbo is not through spelunking—ahead lie the Lonely Mountain and a far more formidable foe than wretched Gollum. Bilbo must now earn his title of burglar—or "expert treasure-hunter," as he would doubtless prefer to be called—by dickering with [the dragon] Smaug the Mighty, "greatest and chiefest of catastrophes." . . .

COMMITTED TO SELF-REALIZATION

Bilbo is terrified. Sting [his sword] and Ring are hardly more than lucky charms in the great treasure cave, not proof against the fearful flamethrower. Smaug is what we of Othello's trade [soldiers] call an area weapon: precise location of the target is not required, nor is fastidious marksmanship necessary for good terminal effect. But Bilbo has guts that belie his species' reputation. None of the Dwarves, not even the venerable, much-decorated Thorin Oakenshield, who proved his mettle in the Goblin Wars, has volunteered to help him burgle treasure with the dragon so near. As he treads the tunnel coming ever nearer to the uninviting red glow the "least Tookish part of him" wavers, wishing yet again for the comfy hole at Bag End.

This is the persona (the "good decent hobbit") railing impotently at the anima (the Tookish part, personified as the great Belladonna, from whom he has surely inherited the

7. Tolkien, *Lord of the Rings*, I: 81.

propensity for disturbing sleeping dragons); but the objections are too little and much too late. He is committed to the path of Self-realization, like it or not. In fact, the controlled social mask is already slipping away, no longer supported by the need to maintain a reputation for the neighbors.

The nature of Bilbo's journey across the landscape of the psyche is revealed by his reply to Smaug's inquiry: "Who are you and where do you come from, if I may ask?"

> "You may indeed! I come from under the hill, and under the hills and over the hills my paths led. And through the air. I am he that walks unseen."

Over hill and under hill, indeed; Bilbo is too modest (if that is possible). "I am the friend of bears and the guest of eagles. I am Ringwinner and Luckwearer."...[8]

This is a complex and pregnant sort of name. It traces his path through conscious and unconscious (over hill and under hill) that has led him this far; establishes his foundation in both worlds ("friend of bears"—i.e., chthonic, earthy, bound to the animal shadow, the instinctive foundation of the psyche; and "guest of eagles"—one who may also soar at will in the light of consciousness). He glories in his new position as pivotal figure in the drama, the link between worlds (Ringwinner) and the key to fortune (Luckwearer) by possession of the magical transcending treasure.

POWERFUL LIBIDO

But Bilbo succumbs to a near fatal weakness at this critical point. He has in the euphoria of the moment reveled too thoughtlessly in Belladonna's triumph, ignored the conscious part of him, which would have been more cautious and circumspect in talking to dragons. Smaug is sure-footed in the dark world, he has dwelt there long; Bilbo is a stranger in the perilous realm, and he has barely stepped into it before the incautious foot is thrust in his mouth, tipping off the worm to dangerous details of the plan. "*Thief* in the *Shadows!*" [O'Neill's italics] snarls the beast, "my armour is like tenfold shields, my teeth are swords, my claws spears, the shock of my tail a thunderbolt, my wings a hurricane, and my breath death!"[9]

This uncouth outburst is one that reveals the volume and fury of the long-repressed libido, the surging, powerful en-

8. Tolkien, *The Hobbit*, p. 213. 9. Ibid., p. 216.

ergy that has for so long been denied conscious symboliza-
tion. Smaug has for the moment ceased to be a transcen-
dental, transforming symbol and become pure animal
power, untamed psychic drive. But transforming symbol is
his major role still, the winged serpent, and like St. George,
Bilbo must slay or outwit the beast to pave the way for the
Self's advent. He has already done this, though he has no
way of knowing it with his careless clues—Smaug is soon up
and around for the first time in years, and Bilbo has provided the clue through the help of the magic thrush that allows Bard the Bowman to finish the monster and quench his
flames. The black arrow pierces the gap in Smaug's armor,
and the treasure is now lying unguarded in the darkness under the mountain.

Now, as Bilbo and the Dwarves begin their greedy inven-
tory of the reclaimed wealth, there is a significant discovery.
Bilbo, unknown to Thorin and company, has found the
Arkenstone, Heart of the Mountain. "Indeed there could not
be two such gems, even in so marvellous a hoard, even in all
the world."[10] It is a perfect crystalline gem, a sparkling pale
globe of light, the most cherished heirloom of the Dwarves
of Erebor.

It is related in symbolism to the *lapis philosophorum*, the
Philosopher's Stone of alchemy, which contains within its
perfect symmetry the means of unifying the opposites, and
means of transforming base metals into gold (also a union of
opposites). In Jungian terms, it is a symbolic realization of
the Self through individuation:

> The goal of individuation, as pictured in unconscious images,
> represents a kind of mid-point or center in which the
> supreme value and the greatest life-intensity are concen-
> trated. It cannot be distinguished from images of the supreme
> values of the various religions. It appears as naturally in the
> individuation process as it does in the religions ... a four-
> square city or garden ... as the *imago Dei* in the soul, as the
> "circle whose periphery is nowhere and whose center is
> everywhere," as a crystal, a stone, a tree, a vessel or a cosmic
> order. ...[11]

Certainly its location, deep in the treasure cave at the
mountain's roots, suggests its abode in the unconscious.
Now it is more than a potential: it, like the Ring, is in Bilbo's
"pocketses."

---

10. Ibid., p. 225. 11. M.L. von Franz, *C.G. Jung, His Myth in Our Time* (Boston: Little
Brown, 1975), pp. 73–74.

It does not remain there long, of course, and Bilbo uses this barter to resolve the political impasse between the Elves and Lakemen on one side and the Dwarves, "under bewilderment of the treasure," on the other. The Arkenstone is both symbol and instrument of his new-found Self; he blends now the pragmatic hobbit of the Shire with the courage and vision of the Tookish adventurer.

Indeed, the little burglar has retrieved more from the dragon's hoard than golden chalices and glittering jewels; his treasure is the treasure of the Self, beside which the wealth of the King under the Mountain, the splendor and worldly pomp and lucre are small change. At the last he has no use for more of this gold than his small measure—enough to be a well-to-do hobbit and live out his life in comfort and contemplation at Bag End (or so he believes). Bilbo Baggins will never be the same. The prosaic gentlehobbit is now poetic as well, his stuffy constricting persona shed (and Old Belladonna silenced), and the realization of his full potential within reach.

"My dear Bilbo!" observes Gandalf. "Something is the matter with you! You are not the hobbit that you were."[12]

12. Tolkien, *The Hobbit*, p. 284.

CHAPTER 2

Meaning in *The Lord of the Rings*

Modern Ideas of Heroism Are a Cornerstone of *The Lord of the Rings*

Roger Sale

Roger Sale examined the portrayal of modern heroism in his book *Modern Heroism: Essays on D.H. Lawrence, William Empson, and J.R.R. Tolkien.* In the following essay, a precursor of that book, Sale argues that despite Tolkien's distaste for his own times, his hero is very much a product of the twentieth century. The portrait of the lonely, scared, but compassionate hero who binds himself to others may partake of all the heroes of the past, but his response is a reaction to the modern world.

In any study of modern heroism, if J.R.R. Tolkien's *The Lord of the Rings* did not exist it would have to be invented. For at one place or another in this massive trilogy all the heroic issues of the western world, from *Beowulf* to D.H. Lawrence, are enacted. . . .

In Tolkien's Middle-earth lie the riders of Rohan, Beowulf-like in their love of lore, their simple and great strength, and their belief that brave men die well in defense of their lord and their honor; Aragorn, half-elven figure of romance, the wandering ranger who becomes King Elessar of Gondor; gigantic Wordsworthian tree-like Ents who swoop down in revenge on the man who treated them wantonly; Sam Gamgee, the namesake of Pickwick's servant, staunch in his servility and love of domesticity; Sam's master, Frodo Baggins, the real hero in this book where all must be heroic, who acts like any modern alienated man but who also is Tolkien's affirmation of possibility in a world where all old and other heroic types are by themselves inadequate. It is, thus, epic and romance and novel by turns, held together by a central myth that manages to partake of all the myths of all the heroes of the past without ever ceasing to be a myth of Tolkien's own devising. . . .

TOLKIEN COULD NOT ESCAPE HIS TIME

For it is Tolkien's lot, just as it has been that of all great writers, to be an historian of his own imagination and to describe the history of his world as he traced his imaginative boundaries. His world, furthermore, is not entirely his own but belongs to us as well, not just because we read him but because we are of his time and his century. Personally perhaps Tolkien would have wished it differently for in much he has written is a great sense of distaste for his own times, and when he has spoken in his own voice (and not as an historian) he can be very harsh:

> Not long ago—incredible though it may seem—I heard a clerk of Oxenford declare that he 'welcomed' the proximity of mass-production robot factories, and the roar of self-obstructive mechanical traffic, because it brought his university into 'contact with real life.' He may have meant that the way men were living and working in the twentieth century was increasing in barbarity at an alarming rate, and that the loud demonstrations of this in the streets of Oxford might serve as a warning that it is not possible to preserve for long an oasis of sanity in a desert of unreason by mere fences, without actual offensive action (practical and intellectual). I fear he did not. In any case the expression 'real life' in this context seems to fall short of academic standards. The notion that motor-cars are more 'alive' than, say, centaurs or dragons is curious; that they are more 'real' than, say, horses is pathetically absurd. ("On Fairy-Stories," in *Essays Presented to Charles Williams* [London, 1947], p. 77)

But fortunately we need not trust the artist when we have such a magnificent tale to trust instead. For Tolkien is not of Middle-earth any more than he is of the germanic dark ages that are his special area of scholastic competence. Willy nilly he belongs to our time, and the more he attempts to ignore or escape this fact the worse he becomes as a writer.

A VERY MODERN HEROISM

William Empson finishes his *Some Versions of Pastoral* with the statement that virtue, intelligence, and good manners are alike lonely and absurd confessions of human limitations. They are, he adds, all the more necessary in our world. That is the idea of modern heroism perhaps most congenial to the liberal spirit, for it accepts the facts of modern life at something like Tolkien's private evaluation of them, and then simply refuses to knuckle under. Empson is a cheerful man, however, and a consistently graceful one, and Tolkien is neither. He is a Christian, not a skeptic, and he believes that the taproot to the past is not yet dried or withered. It would be difficult, therefore, to expect that Tolkien would warm to the idea that his imagination is vastly superior to his theology and that his imagination is of his own time. There are many heroisms in *The Lord of the Rings*, and some are staunch in their commitment to what Empson and many others would consider laughably out of date. Tolkien knows how he wants to reply to their derision, and his defense of his view of the world is careful and polished. But it is, finally, worth rather little because the heroism he writes of best is very modern and even very Empsonian; imagination betrays belief here, as it does so often, yet opens us onto larger worlds too.

For Frodo must try to survive and to win by surviving, and in that case not only valor and physical prowess but the very idea of battles against enemies is not particularly germane. Tolkien has arranged his story so that Sauron cannot openly affect Frodo at all. He binds Frodo only as Frodo binds himself, and Frodo is heroic because he recognizes there is something more important than the question of whether or not he is bound. The landscape of Frodo's great deeds is Sauron's weapon, and for that reason one can call the book Christian and Frodo a pilgrim. But it is a landscape fashioned by the imagination of this century; the wasteland, the valley of ashes, the nightmare cities of [Lawrence's] Rupert Birkin and [Kafka's] Joseph K. What these other authors have tended to think of as the human condition Tolkien finds the grounds for heroic quest, but the circumstances and the atmosphere are the same. He differs from the others primarily because he believes and shows that loneliness, though necessary and unavoidable, is partly a chosen state, the result as much of despair as of the facts of life.

SAM AND SMÉAGOL

It is for this reason that Sam and Sméagol are so important. In their different ways they are better equipped than Frodo to carry the Ring to Mordor. But they are antagonists because imaginatively they are Frodo's inferiors; they cannot trust or sympathize with each other and they cannot understand Frodo's trust and sympathy for them both. Sam feels the power of the Ring only momentarily, and childishly even then, while Sméagol has been totally corrupted by it, and in each case they are protected in a way Frodo cannot be. Sam serves Frodo and Sméagol serves the Ring, but only Frodo serves the heroic idea of the Ring's destruction. If neither is of anything like Frodo's stature, however, he is lost without them. But Frodo knows this and because he knows it can "find" himself in his love for Sam and his compassion for Sméagol and his dependence on them. As long as he is thus dependent, and willingly so, the urge to possessiveness that lies at the heart of the Ring's power to destroy can be combatted. Frodo's virtue lies in his good manners, and his good

---

"My Comment on the World"

When asked to participate in a symposium on children's books to be published in the New Statesman, *Tolkien drafted a long letter in April 1959 explaining why he was declining. He eventually sent only a one-paragraph note of refusal; the following is from the unmailed draft.*

I am not specially interested in children, and certainly not in writing for them: i.e. in addressing directly and expressly those who cannot understand adult language.

I write things that might be classified as fairy-stories not because I wish to address children (who qua children I do not believe to be specially interested in this kind of fiction) but because I wish to write this kind of story and no other.

I do this because if I do not apply too grandiloquent a title to it I find that my comment on the world is most easily and naturally expressed in this way....

I hope 'comment on the world' does not sound too solemn. I have no didactic purpose, and no allegorical intent. (I do not like allegory (properly so called: most readers appear to confuse it with significance or applicability) but that is a matter too long to deal with here.) But long narratives cannot be made out of nothing; and one cannot rearrange the primary matter in secondary patterns without indicating feelings and opinions about one's material.

Humphrey Carpenter, ed., *The Letters of J.R.R. Tolkien.* Boston: Houghton Mifflin, 1981.

manners are his recognition of the blessed and cursed otherness of his servant and his wretched guide.

In a moment of respite on the stairs of Cirith Ungol, before Sméagol takes them to Shelob, Frodo and Sam have a conversation about the songs that will be sung of them after this is all over. Sam does most of the talking, but Frodo makes the key points: 1) "You may know, or guess, what kind of tale it is, happy-ending or sad-ending, but the people in it don't know. And you don't want them to." 2) "No, they never end as tales... but the people in them come, and go, when their parts ended." 3) "Why Sam, to hear you somehow makes me as merry as if the story was already written. But you've left out one of the chief characters: Samwise the stouthearted... and Frodo wouldn't have got far without Sam, would he. . . ." 4) "It's not good to worry about him [Sméagol] now. We couldn't have gotten so far, not even within sight of the pass, without him, and so we'll have to put up with his ways. If he's false, he's false" (II, 321–322).[1] Sam can begin to understand what Frodo is saying, but he cannot by himself rise to the grim and yet almost sublime equipoise of Frodo's weary generosity. But he knows that quality is there in Frodo, as indeed, for a moment, does the Gollum. For after this conversation Frodo and Sam fall asleep and Sméagol discovers them thus, peaceful in each other's arms:

> A strange expression passed over his lean hungry face. The gleam faded from his eyes, and they went dim and grey, old and tired. A spasm of pain seemed to twist him, and he turned away, peering back up towards the pass, shaking his head, as if engaged in some interior debate. Then he came back, and slowly putting out a trembling hand, very cautiously he touched Frodo's knee—but almost the touch was a caress. For a fleeting moment, could one of the sleepers have seen him, they would have thought that they beheld an old weary hobbit, shrunken by the years that carried him far beyond his time, beyond friends and kin, and the fields and streams of youth, an old starved pitiable thing. (II, 324)

This is Sméagol's finest moment, and so, by implication, it is Frodo's finest moment too. Beyond friends and kin, old and tired, Sméagol loves the specialness that is Frodo's care of him. The love is almost without parallel in our modern literature, because it is neither filial nor sexual but the tentative unbelieving response to a caring so unlikely it seems

---

1. Quotations from *The Lord of the Rings* are taken from the revised edition (Boston: Houghton Mifflin, 1967).

heroic even to the Gollum. Whatever might have come afterwards because of this moment is destroyed when Sam wakes up first. He accuses Gollum of being a sneak, and by the time Frodo wakes Sméagol is back to his old whining and sniveling self, ready to lead the hobbits to Shelob.

THE CORNERSTONE OF THE TRILOGY'S GREATNESS

So in a book about hobbits and their return to a world made new, Frodo is the one who can be returned to himself as he sees the light shine in others. Perhaps in Tolkien's official scheme of things this need not seem as important as the original turning out from self to see the world as it is meant to be seen. But still, Frodo finds in this turning out a means to self-knowledge, and in his scarred and beautiful relationship with Sméagol he finds himself and lives by the light of the self he finds. He is saved from the worst ravages of the Ring because he binds himself to others rather than to love of power, and that is his heroism. That is what most profoundly arouses Tolkien's imagination and sympathy too—it may not be what *The Lord of the Rings* is all about and it certainly is not all that it is good for, but it is the cornerstone of its greatness. Over and over in the trilogy we are told of the prices that must be paid when one is called upon to pay them, and with Gandalf, Aragorn, Merry, Pippin, Faramir, the faded elven Kings, and many others we see that such prices are being demanded and paid. But these are ancient heroisms, ancient prices and payments, known and felt to be old and therefore always a trifle artificial, derived, and decorative.

THE HEROISM OF OUR TIME

But this very artificiality is our guide to the genuineness of Frodo's heroism and to our understanding that Tolkien is an historian of heroic acts. For in his Middle-earth, as all the other "great deeds" are chronicled, we respond to that which is most like ourselves because our author so responds too. We see, without in the least needing to make the seeing into a formulation, what the heroism of our time is and can be: lonely, lost, scared, loving, willing, and compassionate—to bind oneself to the otherness of others by recognizing our common livingness. History may create the conditions of chaos, but man's nature is to reply to history as well as to acknowledge it.

Christian Morality in *The Lord of the Rings*

Richard Purtill

The roots of morality and thus of heroism in The
Lord of the Rings *trilogy are deeply planted in Christian tradition, argues Richard Purtill. Critics who
miss the Christian basis of Tolkien's writing, says
Purtill, misunderstand both Christianity and Tolkien.
Purtill is the author of* J.R.R. Tolkien: Myth, Morality,
and Religion *as well as* Lord of the Elves and Eldils,
from which this essay is excerpted.

Both C.S. Lewis and J.R.R. Tolkien . . . are Christians, and
their morality is essentially Christian morality. . . .

Let me now briefly describe Tolkien's world, as many
hints, indirect references, and direct statements give it to us.
Just as in Lewis's space trilogy the state of Earth is supposed
to be the state it is in, and Lewis's secondary world "starts," so
to speak, at the orbit of the moon, so for Tolkien recorded history is supposed to be much as it actually is, and Tolkien's secondary world "starts" before history begins. In both cases
there is some "interpenetration." In [Lewis's *That Hideous*]
Strength the Arthurian legend becomes history, and in
Tolkien it is suggested that elves, hobbits, and other creatures
linger on into recorded history. But before recorded history
there are certain events which Tolkien, as a Christian, holds
to have actually occurred—for instance, the fall of man. Thus,
since there are men in Tolkien's story, they must be fallen
men; the Fall is in the *past* of Tolkien's world. And, of course,
the men in the story of the Ring are obviously fallen men.

What about the other races? Not being "sons of Adam," they
are not necessarily fallen; they may be like Lewis's Malacandrans or Perelandrans. And, in fact, there are some analogies
between Lewis's "races" and Tolkien's. Let me first give a table
of my proposed correspondences, and then defend it.

Excerpted from *Lord of the Elves and Eldils: Fantasy and Philosophy in C.S. Lewis and
J.R.R. Tolkien,* by Richard Purtill (Grand Rapids, MI: Zondervan, 1974). Reprinted by
permission of the author. (Footnotes in the original have been adapted in this reprint.)

Tolkien's	correspond to	Lewis's
Elves (wizards)	"	Good eldils (Oyarses)
Dwarves (ents?)	"	Malacandrans
Orcs, trolls (Sauron)	"	"Bent" eldils (The "Bent One")

Elves and orcs are unlike eldils in that eldils are purely spiritual beings. (But the function of elves in Tolkien's story is like that of eldils in Lewis's trilogy as, for example, Tom Bombadil's function is rather like Merlin's in *Strength*.) Elves are like eldils in being confirmed in goodness or badness; there is no such thing as an evil elf of a good orc in Tolkien. Ents are evidently not confirmed in goodness like elves. Treebeard says of his people,

> "I do not understand all that goes on myself, so I cannot explain it to you. Some of us are still true Ents, and lively enough in our fashion, but many are growing sleepy, going treeish, as you might say. Most of the trees are just trees, of course; but many are half awake. Some are quite wide awake, and a few are, well, ah, well getting *Entish*. That is going on all the time.
>
> "When that happens to a tree, you find that some have *bad* hearts. Nothing to do with their wood: I do not mean that. Why, I knew some good old willows down the Entwash, gone long ago, alas! They were quite hollow, indeed they were falling all to pieces, but as quiet and sweet-spoken as a young leaf. And then there are some trees in the valleys under the mountains, sound as a bell, and bad right through. That sort of thing seems to spread. There used to be some very dangerous parts in this country. There are still some very black patches."

However, the ents have an "anti-race," like the elves. Treebeard says, "Maybe you have heard of Trolls? They are mighty strong. But Trolls are only counterfeits, made by the Enemy in the Great Darkness in mockery of Ents, as Orcs were of Elves." This may suggest that trolls and orcs are actually *created* by the Enemy, but elsewhere Gandalf denies that the Enemy can create; he can only spoil and corrupt. In fact, "Nothing is evil in the beginning. Even Sauron was not so," which suggests that he is, like Satan, a fallen being of great power.

Dwarves, like the Malacandrans, seem to be basically good, but there seems to be a possibility of individual falls; an evil dwarf is not an impossibility. And Gimli the dwarf in some way rises above his dwarvish destiny, becoming a sort of adopted elf.

Hobbits pose a special problem, and here I indulge in a bit of speculation which might have been entirely rejected by Tolkien himself. All that he himself says is that

> it is plain indeed that Hobbits are relatives of ours: far nearer to us than Elves, or even than Dwarves. Of old they spoke the languages of Men, after their own fashion, and liked and disliked much the same things as Men did. But what exactly our relationship is can no longer be discovered.

However, the hobbits are continually referred to as "halflings," a term Tolkien explains as "half the size of a grown man." Can there also be some suggestion here of half-*breeds?* Can the hobbits in fact be the offspring of an interbreeding of two other races? If so, which two? Not elves and men. The offspring of such unions appear in the story in the persons of Elrond and Aragorn, and they are quite unlike hobbits. I once thought hobbits might be the offspring of an elf-dwarf cross and connected in some way with the "old quarrel" between elves and dwarves. Gimli falls in love with Galadriel (in a remote and chivalric way, it is true, yet she is a sort of elvish saint or superwoman and he is not correspondingly great). What if some dwarvish king or warrior had fallen in love with a more eccessible elf-maiden and carried her off? Might this not have led to a spreading quarrel (Helen of Troy long before Troy), and might not the offspring of such a union, perhaps intermarrying with other dwarves, have founded a new race who found it best to vanish quietly into a remote corner of the world?

I still think this possible, from what Tolkien tells us of his world, but I am now inclined to think that a mixed dwarf-human ancestry is more plausible in view of the part hobbits play in the story. For, if hobbits are partly human, much is explained: the fact that they have no language of their own but speak that of men; their resemblances to both men and dwarves in certain respccts; and, above all, the vital role they play in the process in which the Third Age—the age of many "speaking races"—comes to an end, and the Fourth Age—the age of man—begins.

A CONSTANT MORAL STRUGGLE

Be this as it may, the real moral focus of Tolkien's story is on the two races, hobbits and men. They can sink to complete damnation, as the Ringwraiths have done, and as Bilbo or Frodo might have. But they can rise to something like sanctity, as Frodo does. We have detailed pictures of moral struggle in men (Boromir, Théoden, Denethor), in most of the hobbit characters (especially Frodo, Sam, and Bilbo, but also Merry and Pippin), and in the wizard Saruman who is at least ostensibly a man or elf-man.

The constant temptation of all the characters is to give in, give up the struggle and cooperate with the Dark Lord. Against this the virtues characteristic of the heroes of the story are courage, will and endurance, and loyalty and love. We see the first sketch of this in Bilbo, hero of *The Hobbit.* At the beginning of the story he is seemingly a fussy, self-important little man (not middle-aged; that is a mistake which arises from applying human time-scales to longer-lived creatures). Partly by clever pressure from Gandalf, partly from injured vanity, he commits himself to an adventure with Thorin and his dwarves. As the dangers start, he begins to find his courage, first trying to pick a troll's pocket (with disastrous results), then giving the alarm during the capture by the goblins. Lost in the flight from the goblins after Gandalf rescues the troop, Bilbo meets Gollum and outwits him in the dark, finds his magic ring and begins to use it. In the forest he saves the dwarves from the giant spiders, aided by a magic ring and an elvish blade, but showing a great deal of courage and resourcefulness. He rescues the dwarves from the Elven-king's dungeons, but the real test of his courage is when he twice faces Smaug, the great dragon, gaining the knowledge that enables Bard, the hero, to kill the villain.

At the end of the tale, however, Bilbo shows his real stature. Faced with the refusal of the dwarves to share their wealth with the townsfolk against whom they aroused the dragon, and whose captain slew the dragon, Bilbo determines to see justice done. He gives the Arkenstone to the Elf-king and Bard to bargain with, then goes back to face the wrath of the dwarves. Love of justice and love of peace here raise Bilbo to a height not far below Frodo, the Ring-bearer.

FRODO ACTS FOR THE SAKE OF OTHERS

Frodo rises to greater heights because from the beginning he accepts the burden of the Ring purely for the sake of others. It is no mere adventure that sends Frodo riding out of the Shire, but a willingness to suffer so that others may be saved—a willingness which is tested to the last grim degree on the black plains of Mordor. Frodo is not Christ, the Ring is not the Cross, and the salvation his sacrifice wins is a purely secular salvation. But there are obviously echoes of these greater realities in the fictional "Passion" of Frodo. "Greater love has no man than this, that a man lay down his life for his friends," says Christ, and Frodo's journey is at least an illustration of this.

The growth of Frodo in courage and loyalty is clear enough as the story develops. At the first real test, in the den of the Barrow-wight, he is tempted to use the Ring to save himself.

> A wild thought of escape came to him. He wondered if he put on the Ring whether the Barrow-wight would miss him, and he might find some way out. He thought of himself running free over the grass, grieving for Merry, Sam, and Pippin, but free and alive himself.[1]

He rejects the temptation and begins to grow toward his final stature. There are other crises, and the Ring itself betrays him several times. But he is able to resist the call of the Ringwraiths to surrender on Weathertop and at the Ford of Bruinen, and to make up his own mind when assailed by the enemy on Amon Hen.

> . . . suddenly he felt the Eye. There was an eye in the Dark Tower that did not sleep. He knew that it had become aware of his gaze. A fierce eager will was there. It leaped towards him; almost like a finger he felt it, searching for him. Very soon it would nail him down, know just exactly where he was. Amon Lhaw it touched. It glanced upon Tol Brandir—he threw himself from the seat, crouching, covering his head with his grey hood.
>
> He heard himself crying out: *Never, never!* Or was it: *Verily I come, I come to you?* He could not tell. Then as a flash from some other point of power there came to his mind another thought: *Take it off! Take it off! Fool, take it off! Take off the Ring!*
>
> The two powers strove in him. For a moment, perfectly balanced between their piercing points, he writhed, tormented. Suddenly he was aware of himself again. Frodo, neither the Voice nor the Eye: free to choose, and with one remaining instant in which to do so. He took the Ring off his finger. He was kneeling in clear sunlight before the high seat. A black shadow seemed to pass like an arm above him; it missed Amon Hen and groped out west, and faded. Then all the sky was clean and blue and birds sang in every tree.[2]

Frodo grows even greater as he journeys on with Sam and Gollum. His gentleness to Gollum almost conquers the crea-

---

1. J.R.R. Tolkien, *The Fellowship of the Ring,* rev. ed. (New York: Ballantine Books, 1969), p. 195. 2. Ibid., p. 519.

ture's withered heart, and his steady endurance of his burden as it grows almost overwhelming contains a moving echo of the Way of the Cross. Indeed, his nightmare journey across the blasted plains of Mordor with Sam and Gollum tends sometimes to dominate our memory of the book, so that it is easy to forget how much laughter and enchantment and delight the story contains. . . .

THE RING HAS SATANIC POWER

It may be well here to clear up a minor misunderstanding about the Ring itself. It has been blithely identified with Power by both friendly and unfriendly critics. Mary Ellman accused Tolkien's characters of being afraid of power, and even some of his admirers talk merely about the "dangers of power." But, of course, the Ring has not merely neutral power, but satanic power: the Dark Lord "has put a great part of his own power into it," and this is why its destruction does more than deprive Sauron of *more* power—it destroys him. When Gandalf and Galadriel refuse the Ring, it is not because "power corrupts"; they are, apart from Sauron, the most powerful persons in the story. Rather, they rejected it because using the Ring to do good would be attempting to use Satan's power to do good, and this will inevitably defeat the good purpose and turn it to evil.

Saruman tries to tempt Gandalf with the power of the Ring and the plea that the end justifies the means.

> ". . . listen, Gandalf, my old friend and helper!" he said, coming near and speaking now in a softer voice. "I said *we*, for *we* it may be, if you will join with me. A new Power is rising. Against it the old allies and policies will not avail us at all. There is no hope left in Elves or dying Numenor. This then is once choice before you, before us. We may join with that Power. It would be wise, Gandalf. There is hope that way. Its victory is at hand; and there will be rich reward for those that aided it. As the Power grows, its proved friends will also grow; and the Wise, such as you and I, may with patience come at last to direct its courses, to control it. We can bide our time, we can keep our thoughts in our hearts, deploring maybe evils done by the way, but approving the high and ultimate purpose: Knowledge, Rule, Order; all the things that we have so far striven in vain to accomplish, hindered rather than helped by our weak or idle friends. There need not be, there would not be any real change in our designs, only in our means."[3]

Both in the case of Saruman and in the case of Gollum,

3. Ibid., p. 340.

there is a sense that there may be a real possibility of their redemption. When Gandalf pleads with Saruman after his defeat, Saruman wavers for a moment. Just before Gollum betrays Frodo, he almost gives in to love for him. Each being in the story is good or evil by his own choice, and that choice is a genuinely free one, though powerful forces from inside and out attempt to influence it. As Gandalf says of Gollum:

> "Even Gollum was not wholly ruined. He had proved tougher than even one of the Wise would have guessed—as a hobbit might. There was a little corner of his mind that was still his own, and light came through it, as through a chink in the dark: light out of the past. It was actually pleasant, I think, to hear a kindly voice again, bringing up memories of wind, and trees, and sun on the grass, and such forgotten things.

> "But that, of course, would only make the evil part of him angrier in the end—unless it could be conquered. Unless it could be cured." Gandalf sighed "Alas! there is little hope of that for him. Yet not no hope. No, not though he possessed the Ring so long, almost as far back as he can remember. For it was long since he had worn it much: in the black darkness it was seldom needed. Certainly he had never 'faded.' He is thin and tough still. But the thing was eating up his mind, of course, and the torment had become almost unbearable."[4]

. . . The responsibility of each person to do God's work, the danger of using evil means—this is Tolkien's message.

---

4. Ibid., pp. 86–87.

A Grand Adventure but a Dangerous Blueprint for Human Affairs

Kenneth McLeish

Scholars debate the source of the morality in *The Lord of the Rings*, but generally suggest that, whatever its basis, if humans would return to the hierarchical rural decency Tolkien depicts, all would once again be right with the world, charges Kenneth McLeish. McLeish examines the influences of popular culture and mass fiction of Tolkien's time and concludes that *The Lord of the Rings* is permeated with a dangerously shallow view of human affairs and a disturbing attachment to the values of the Victorian era. Read the trilogy for great entertainment, he urges, but not for a blueprint for society. McLeish is author or editor of several dozen books, including one on the complete myths and legends of the Greeks, *Children of the Gods*.

YIN AND YANG

A clue to the essential nature of *The Lord of the Rings* is the almost total absence of femininity. I don't just mean that we hear nothing of Mrs. Gandalf, Merry's girl-friends (he surely wasn't a Brandybuck for nothing) or the home life of our own dear Wormtongue (was Mrs. Gríma a shrew—or nagged to shreds?). I don't mean that the few female characters we *do* hear about are cardboard figures from Welsh legend (like the ineffable Arwen, who was, if you'll pardon Tolkien's prose, 'so like in form of womanhood to Elrond that Frodo guessed she was one of his close kindred') or knockabout comediennes from the Victorian stage (*The Wooing of Sam and Rosie Gamgee* would surely have rolled 'em

Excerpted from Kenneth McLeish, "The Rippingest Yarn of All," in *J.R.R. Tolkien: This Far Land*, edited by Robert Giddings. Copyright © 1983 Vision Press Ltd. Reprinted by permission of A.P. Watt Ltd. on behalf of Valerie McLeish.

in the aisles. . . .) By absence of femininity I meant the lack of any true gentleness, grace or what the Oxford dictionary calls 'passivity' in the characters, of any vision of behavior beyond gruff comradeship (or its mirror sycophancy), bully-boy rant (or its mirror fortitude) and, to remind us now and then that our heroes are really just like us, the brushing away of a furtive but manly tear. . . .

Homer's *Iliad*, an epic which *does* include the feminine, hinges on the quarrel between Agamemnon (the masculine principle in nature, or *yang*, personified) and Achilles (the feminine principle, or *yin*) over a captured princess; its climactic battle (between Achilles and another yangy male, Hector) is not only preceded by one of the most moving 'feminine' scenes in literature, the farewell between Hector, Andromache and their baby son (who is terrified by his father's overshadowing helmet-plumes), but is followed by another, in which Priam pitifully pleads with the Greeks for Hector's corpse. Homer's *Odyssey*, the 'quest' narrative to end them all, charts Odysseus' growth not only as he comes to terms with every conceivable variety of female (calculating Calypso, nymphet Nausicaa, Marlene-Dietrich Circe), but more importantly as he realizes that the gentle and pliable qualities in his own nature are strength, not weakness, and as he persuades first his wife Penelope and then his people that because he has changed, has united the warring aspects in his own nature, he is worthy at last to be Penelope's husband and his people's king.

Where is this kind of profundity in *The Lord of the Rings*? Do its characters grow, in yin-and-yang harmonization or in any other way? Boromir, to be sure, learns that he is as greedy for the Ring as anyone else, that he is not the gentil parfit knight he thought himself; Frodo is revealed more and more as 'the outsider' (Camus, and Sartrean existentialism, were much in the air as Tolkien wrote); Gandalf turns from grey to white convincingly enough to pass the strictest window-test. But this is declaration of character, not growth: in each case it reveals only what was latent from the start. Like a preacher, Tolkien first tells us what his moral lessons are going to be, then goes through them painstakingly one by one. The dwarves become more dwarfish, the elves more elvish, the orcs more orc-like, even the hobbits more hobbity. The underlying moral messages are 'Discover your true self, and be true to it', and—less creditably—'Be wary of anyone Not Like

Us.' I think only the kindly old Ents avoid such pragmatic chauvinism—and all even they ever want is to be left alone.

Comparing Tolkien with Homer—as Tolkien would have been the first to point out—is pompous and silly. All he claimed to be doing was producing 'mythologies', extending his plunderings of the Red Book, already used in *The Hobbit* (his masterpiece, because it never aspires to allegorical significance, and is therefore superbly self-consistent); he nevertheless pointed out that

> since my children and others of their age, who first heard of the finding of the Ring, have grown older with the years, this book speaks more plainly of those darker things which lurked only on the borders of the earlier tale, but which troubled Middle-Earth in all its history.

It speaks of them all, that is, except—as J. W. Lambert pointed out when he first reviewed the book—except for God and sex. Leaving God aside for the moment, let's consider sex. Is there, somewhere in the morass of material which might have constituted *Silmarillion II* (and still might: *there's* a thought) Tolkien's *Tristan and Isolde*, his solution to the problems of uniting yin and yang? Or was *The Lord of the Rings* intended from the start as no more than an adult *Hobbit*, a fairy-tale for grown-up people?—in which case, like all half way decent tale-tellers (Bilbo himself states as much), if a particular aspect of experience didn't suit Tolkien's story, he left it out. Fair enough. But for those who claim higher status for *The Lord of the Rings* than that of a simple tale, the absence of sex—to say nothing of its benign transfiguration, love—is a matter to be reckoned with.

UPMARKET AND DOWN

Grown-ups, writing tales for children (and for other grown-ups): those are the key factors. What other tales might Tolkien himself, or his children, have experienced? What was a chap (or a chap's friend) likely to be reading in the 1900s, or in the 1930s (when Tolkien himself started publishing children's books, and presumably sniffed out the market first)? On what well-established foundations, in short, on what familiar ground, was the edifice of his life's work laid down?

I stress that I'm not talking about things like *Beowulf*, the *Kalevala* or the *Mabinogion*, the material Tolkien and his friends loved reading aloud to each other over mugs of ale. This kind of source-material is well documented elsewhere (and the documents should be known to every self-respecting Tolkien enthusiast. *A propos*, has anyone noticed the links between his work and Hermann Hesse's *Narcissus and Gold-mund* or *The Glass Bead Game*? Worth looking up.) I'm talking about popular literature, mass fiction, the furniture of the growing mind which we all take for granted as we grow, which helps our growing and which we generally put aside as soon as we've grown.

Curiously, this brings us straight back to God, to that other element crucial to literary stature which is missing from *The Lord of the Rings* (because it consistently confuses the metaphysical with the supernatural). The first inkling comes from the writings of Tolkien's donnish colleague and friend C. S. Lewis. Lewis was much concerned with metaphysics, with the Problem of Good and Evil (the capitals—and the simplification of the issue—are his), and produced a clutch of books (notably *The Screwtape Letters*) depicting the quest of and for the human soul in the form of a kind of Shavian fishing-manual, full of urbane jokes and shallow-profound metaphorical advice—'Whatever you do, don't cast where God is, or you'll foul your line.' He also wrote a legend-cycle for children, the *Narnia* books, which Tolkien heartily disliked and in which Good heroically and interminably battles Bad. But the clue lies less in any of these works than in his three remarkable science-fiction novels for adults, the first of which, *Out of the Silent Planet*, was published in 1938, just before *The Hobbit*. (Like Tolkien, Lewis went on in subsequent books, *Perelandra* and *That Hideous Strength*, to darken and broaden an originally simple theme.)

Out of the Silent Planet starts with a lone walker in a leafy, placid Shire, who can't find a pub and calls instead at a lonely house. Here he meets someone, a 'slender man' (the adjective is fanged) who claims to be a fellow spirit ('"By Jove," said the slender man, "Not Ransome who used to be at Wedenshaw?"'), and takes him for a ride and on a quest on which ultimately the whole future of the race depends. Like Bilbo in *The Hobbit*, Lewis's nudgingly-named Ransome travels with strange companions to very strange places; like Bilbo, he triumphs in the end over terrible evil by a mixture of ruefulness, determination and muddling through; like Bilbo, he is forever changed by his experience.

The difference is that Lewis's hero journeys not overland to Misty Mountains and beyond, but through space to Mars. *Out of the Silent Planet,* for all its overtones of Christian redemption and of decency and honesty fighting the fascist beast—overtones which Lewis, like Tolkien later with *The Lord of the Rings,* strenuously and disingenuously disclaimed—is an H. G. Wells science-fiction tale made over for a darker age. The traveller is a middle-class 'loner'; his 'slender' companion is at his least trustworthy when he smiles; mysterious, attractive beings are met *en route,* and reluctantly abandoned; there is an all-important battle and a sad aftermath. This is *Hobbit* country, but it is also the well-charted territory favoured by the literate Edwardian middle class.

Lewis is a far worse writer than Tolkien, chiefly because he lets his moral messages overburden his prose. But whatever its quality, *Out of the Silent Planet* reminds us how much *The Lord of the Rings* also owes to H.G. Wells. One example, in particular, leaps out of Tolkien's narrative. When Frodo, Sam and Gollum finally begin struggling up Mount Doom, the landscape, in its mixture of desolation, devastation and threat, seems uncannily familiar. It's not the Brecon Beacons, the Peak District or the Scottish Highlands (much too sinister); it's not even modelled on those shattered, barren vistas we all known as a fall-out from twentieth-century war. The impression that you've been there before arises because you *have,* in Wells's *The War of the Worlds,* first published in 1898, and a best-seller for ten years (i.e. all through Tolkien's adolescence). In this book, Martians and earthmen face each other for the final battle on just such scorched, bleak and above all menacing terrain. Wells could have been in the back of Tolkien's mind as he wrote *The Hobbit,* too: the terrifying film of *Things to Come* was issued in 1936, and its reputation would have reached even the most kinematophobic Oxford don, as it occasioned Questions in the House [British Parliament] and even Letters to *The Times* [of London]. There was a fine film of *The War of the Worlds* in 1953, two years before the publication of *The Return of the King.* Still another Wells story, *The Island of Doctor Moreau* (again hugely popular during Tolkien's adolescence) is about ugly, satanic and pitiable creatures, animal/human hybrids produced by vivisection and genetic manipulation. One of the most striking of them all (the puma-creature) has large, pale eyes, grasping bony hands and hissing speech. . . .

We shall never know if Tolkien consciously imitated (or even remembered) Wells; but clearly the man was around at the crucial time to strike sparks in Tolkien's adolescent mind. So was the masterpiece of another fine writer, Kenneth Grahame, whose *The Wind in the Willows* (first published in 1908, when Tolkien was 16) could be found on every middle-class child's bookshelf for three generations, a superb (if daunting) model for any aspiring writer of children's fantasy. There's no need to rehearse the similarities in detail—the description of Mole's house at the beginning, the gargantuan meals, Toad's Sackville-Bagginsy social pretension, Badger's twinkly-eyed crustiness (so like Gandalf's)—but two sections in particular are close to Tolkien in both spirit and style. The chapter at the end, in which all the nasty creatures from the Wild Wood are routed, is described with the same panache as Tolkien uses for Merry's or Pippin's adventures with the orcs . . . ; and the chapter in *The Wind in the Willows* which I always found baffling as a child, in which the animals hear distant pan-pipes and are transported into a kind of rural trance, an ecstatic revelling in the sounds, smells, feel and psychic peacefulness of nature, is remarkably like what happens to Frodo and his friends when they stay with the Elves, and is told in that archly suggestive, Dante-Gabriel-Rossetti style—writing about magic trances was once as embarrassing to English authors as discussing sex or metaphysics—which is the hallmark of all Edwardian writing involving nature-mysticism, from the twee mythological rehashings of Andrew Lang to the poems of Walter de la Mare and the plays of Barrie (about whose *Peter Pan* Tolkien wrote in his 1910 diary 'indescribable, but shall never forget it as long as I live').

Wells, Grahame and Barrie: for many of those of us who passed our childhood and adolescence in the 1930s and 1940s, those are potent names. We learned from them that there was a world outside our own, much less comfortable and inhabited by unpredictable and often monstrous mutations of our own kind; we learned that our own world was safe and desirable, and could, if we used ingenuity and courage, be saved from outside threat. (It needs no palantír to see more anti-fascist implications here.) We're not quite in Tolkien territory—dignity and elevation of style are missing—but we're getting close.

OUR SORT

The over-simplification of moral issues in Wells, Grahame or Barrie was self-declaring and harmless, and made their work a wholesome tonic for the growing mind: silly enough to see through, but serious enough at least to raise the problems that perplex the young. A far more insidious, and far more sinister, influence comes in another type of children's literature, embodied in Tolkien's boyhood by the public-school sagas of Talbot Baines Reed and the adventure stories of Captain Marryat or G.A. Henty, and in his children's childhood by the messing-about-in-boats yarns of Arthur Ransome on the one hand, and on the other the 'he smiled grimly as the Boche spun out of control to his well-earned doom' tales of Percy F. Westerman and the unspeakable (but readable) Captain W.E. Johns. For adults, exactly the same philosophies were persuasively peddled in the 1910s and 1920s by Sapper, Edgar Wallace, Dornford Yates and their ilk, and in the 1930s and 1940s by what Colin Watson memorably christened the 'snobbery with violence' school of detective fiction whose joint headmistresses were Agatha Christie and the learned but muddle-headed Dorothy L. Sayers.

This literature is dangerous because it takes all ethical or moral problems for granted, as part of a desirable *status quo* which the villains constantly challenge and the heroes constantly reaffirm. Without exception, it hymns the British Imperial certainties of Tolkien's youth, a time when no one except foreigners like Freud and Marx—seriously 'got in the way of things'. Society, by and large, worked well—and it was sturdily structured on the premise that everyone knew his place. Women's place, for example, was firmly at home, queening it at tea beside the buddleia or scrubbing and scrimping behind the scenes; the few eccentrics who chained themselves to railings or chaired Fabian Society meetings were regarded by everyone else (including the majority of their own sex) as 'unladylike', 'beyond the pale'. The Lower Orders were servile or perky to a man—and the extent of their servility or perkiness depended on their employers' whim. Even within the ruling class there were Those who Decided and Those who Agreed: in real life, the Cabinet formulated policy and the Whips ensured that the House of Commons enacted it; in popular literature every Raffles, Berry or Holmes had a devoted but flea-brained sidekick, and Wimsey, Poirot and their rivals delighted in outsmarting everyone in sight; even in the public-school dorms and studies of *Stalky and Co.* or on Ballantyne's notorious *Coral Island* there were patrol-leader types and the

Good Scouts they led.

Outside this charmed circle, as everyone knew . . . , but as only troublemakers like Wells and Shaw kept pointing out, there was a vast, inarticulate army who maintained the edifice: the factory-workers, labourers, salesmen and shopgirls of country towns. They surfaced every five years (males over 21, at least) to vote at elections; but Parliament was reliably a talking-shop, and real government was carried on discreetly and imperturbably by a civil service as silkily irreplaceable as a first-class family retainer, and by the occasional, essential derring-do of aristocratic loners. It was Ruritania, happy and glorious; it was Tolkien's Shire. Only when the inarticulate army of the suburbs became the all-too-visible (and embarrassingly dead) army of the War to End Wars [World War I] was the Edwardian British twilight seen at last for what it was, the genteel decadence of a once thriving and invincible force.

It is my view that the books of Yates, Sayers and their like—favourite reading, we are assured, of the governing class—dangerously carried this shallow view of affairs, this smug or brainless clinging to the ethical verities of a vanished Victorian era, into the wholly alien decades of the first world war, the Depression and the General Strike—and that *The Lord of the Rings* still perpetuates them in an (even less appropriate) era of mass democracy on the one hand and the imminent possibility of a nuclear apocalypse on the other. The view—which had once been true—that 'all that sort of thing can be left to Our Betters' or to 'Those Who Know about Such Things' underlies every page of *The Lord of the Rings*, an indication of how far in the establishment past its author's view of affairs was formed, and of how little it had been shaken by Mosley, the Spanish Civil War, the abdication, Chamberlain, by the aristocratic oafs who generalled and air-marshalled Britain through the Phoney War (till Churchill, that visionary ostracized for a dozen years by his own caste, was plummeted into power), and by Dachau, Hiroshima and the closing of the Iron Curtain (all events predating *The Lord of the Rings*, and proving that the world was a bigger and far more dangerous place than placid Oxfordshire, and could never be so scaled-down again).

There are those who claim that all this turmoil *is* reflected in *The Lord of the Rings*, that the message underlying it is that if only humanity would return to a species of hierarchical rural decency (but never religious—God is, as I have said, rigorously excluded from Tolkien's cosmology), all might again be well. There are, Tolkien says somewhere, many people who know nothing of Frodo's and Sam's adventure, but who are able to sleep more easily in their beds because it has taken place. I would suggest two things: first, that carrying a Ring to dump into a volcano against all odds, helped by a representative of every species (a League of Nations with a constitution borrowed from the Icelandic sagas), and rescued at crisis-points by coincidence (Gwaihir the Windlord, yet!), by magic or by blundering-through (the climax on Mount Doom is a glorious, shambolic *mess*, one of the very few places in the whole epic where Tolkien contrives even a twitch of irony at his characters' expense)—I would suggest that this is a very poor allegory for how we should run our century, and second, that it was precisely this Edwardianly cosy view of human affairs in real life that cost Britain its Empire, cost Europe millions upon millions of its young men, and, unless we abandon it right now, will quite possibly cost us this planet and everything on it.

THE QUALITY OF TOLKIEN

... For the reasons outlined above (among others) I don't think Tolkien is an epic writer to compare with Homer, and I find his mythopoeic view of life too restricted, too simplistic, to stand up against the moral truths, meticulous observation and metaphysical profundity of the finest novelists (e.g. Balzac, Mann or Proust). The cult that has mushroomed round his imagined world is as dottily devoted, and ultimately as frivolous (because remote from reality) as those endless genealogies of invented races and grammars of made-up languages that stuffed Tolkien's own mind and plump up even his minor work. I think that the vision of society put forward in *The Lord of the Rings* is old-fashioned, wrong-headed and a lethal model for late twentieth-century living, as likely to succeed as the wooden rifles and bean-poles with which Dad's Army once hoped to keep the invading Hun at bay. To put it bluntly, we live in a nasty, dangerous and brutal world, and dressing up in elven-cloaks, baking lembas and writing poems in Entish, though a commendable and delightful game, is a way of avoiding, not finding, the truth of life.

So where does that leave Tolkien? If those of his cultists who take him seriously are dangerously deluded, does that necessarily make him a fool as well? Of course not. The time has come to lay my cards on the table and say that I think Tolkien was one of the finest writers of escapist fantasy in any language and of any time. (Homer, Tolstoy, Dickens, aren't in competition. Their subject was reality.) His verse may be appalling, his prose convoluted and often arch, and his inspiration a magpie's nest of half-remembered instances from every piece of literature he ever read, from *King Lear* to *Noddy in Toyland.* But he hooks you from the first sentence, and drags you gasping and sighing through every spiral of his narrative, leaving you always hungry, always wanting more. The Quest is one of the surest of all fictional plots. It has a clearly marked start and a clearly defined end—and this clarity allows for all manner of diversions, twists and turns *en route.* In Tolkien's landscape every stone and tree has a part to play and a story to tell—indeed trees come to life and *tell* their stories. His world is full of wonders; magic is not special, but particular to everyone. Any author who invents Moria, Rivendell, the Ringwraiths, my own favourites the Ents, Gandalf and Saruman, is a storyteller to reckon with—and when he goes on to detail his fantasy with whole cycles of history, whole geographies, whole languages, how can we not be charmed? Tolkien's world, unlike the real world of infinite possibility in which we live, offers the attractions of completeness: he has anticipated every question and found an answer before you asked.

If your work is a magpie's hoard, what matters for greatness is the use you make of the glittering jewels you find—and this, I suggest, is the main facet of Tolkien's genius. He keeps reminding us of other things, stirring our memory of books, images and ideas we'd long forgotten; but he gives each memory, each allusion, a new twist and so redoubles its power. (Well, not always. The whole Theoden episode is a very faint echo of the hero-sagas from which it derives: try *Beowulf,* or consider what Wagner—whom Tolkien so heartily despised—did with Nordic mythology in *his The Ring.*) The underground sequences are brilliantly brought off, the finest portions of the book; the Balrog, Shelob and above all Gollum are both persuasive delineations of evil and creepily credible as characters; the Ents (though their origin could be unkindly traced to Enid Blyton's *The Faraway Tree* and their siege of Isengard, as recounted by Merry . . . , to Hesiod's version of the Earthborn Giants' attack on the Olympian gods) are a spectacular creation, as convincing a metaphor for the force and dignity of nature as Bombadil is a plastic one. And, most striking of all, Tolkien's careful blend of tones of voice—he moves in a paragraph from the down-to-earthness of the Hobbits (all grumbling bellies and hamster-like alarm) to the 'Lo! how brave the banners blew' alliterative-epic nonsense of the Rohirrim, the stabbing gutturals of the orcs, the hooming and homming of the Ents and the hissing duplicity of Gríma and Sméagol—all this gives the story forward movement, pace, and that essential ingredient of all good yarns, unexpectedness: you *have* to turn each page to see what horrors or delights are lurking there.

So, from the great cycles of saga and from the far less elevated but no less evocative tales that helped to form his and our youth, Tolkien assembles a hundred ideas, a thousand strands of narrative, and weaves them into a single, glowing tapestry, a work which reveals not only the capacious literary ragbag that was his mind, but also his genius for organization and redeployment. He is like a museum curator, with exhibits from all the world's cultures arranged to give maximum delight. And if—as I have suggested—a major part of his collection consists of pages torn from the children's or grown-ups' escapist adventure-stories of the twentieth century, what he has written beggars all his sources, and—providing we never take it as any kind of answer to the world's problems—is stunningly readable, breathtakingly exciting and morally unambiguous: in short, the ripping yarn to end them all.

Charges of Racism in *The Lord of the Rings* Are Mistaken

Patrick Curry

Tolkien has been accused of being an English chauvinist, of trying to perpetuate divisions between classes, even of being a racist, reports Patrick Curry. While the hobbits are to a large degree a self-portrait of the English, readers will connect them with rustic peoples anywhere in the world. As to charges against Tolkien of bias and bigotry, Curry points out that class awareness in the trilogy merely reflects modern reality; moreover, "interracial" marriage and friendships between members of different races assert "the wonder of multicultural difference" rather than any sort of apartheid. Curry is the author of *Defending Middle-Earth: Tolkien, Myth and Modernity*, from which this essay is excerpted.

It is as neighbours, full of ineradicable prejudices, that we must love each other, and not as fortuitously 'separated brethren.'[1]

Hobbits, according to Tolkien, were more frequent 'long ago in the quiet of the world. . . .' They 'love peace and quiet and good tilled earth: a well-ordered and well-farmed countryside was their favourite haunt. They do not and did not understand or like machines more complicated than a forge-bellows, a water-mill, or a hand-loom. . . . Their faces were as a rule good-natured rather than beautiful, broad, bright-eyed, red-cheeked, with mouths apt to laughter, and to eating and drinking.' They thought of themselves as 'plain quiet folk' with 'no use for adventures. Nasty disturbing uncomfortable things! Make you late for dinner!' 'Nonetheless,' their chronicler notes, 'ease and peace had left this people

Excerpted from *Defending Middle-Earth: Tolkien, Myth and Modernity,* by Patrick Curry. Copyright © 1997 by Patrick Curry. Reprinted with permission from St. Martin's Press, Inc.

still curiously tough. They were, if it came to it, difficult to daunt or to kill. . . .' In other words, they manifested 'the notorious Anglo-hobbitic inability to know when they're beaten.'[2]

Hobbits were also inclined 'to joke about serious things,' and 'say less than they mean.' Indeed, they 'will sit on the edge of ruin and discuss the pleasures of the table, or the small doings of their fathers, grandfathers, and great-grandfathers, and remoter cousins to the ninth degree, if you encourage them with undue patience.' Similarly, they preferred speeches that were 'short and obvious,' and 'liked to have books filled with things that they already knew, set out fair and square with no contradictions.' They were 'a bit suspicious . . . of anything out of the way—uncanny, if you understand me.'[3] It wasn't difficult to acquire a reputation for peculiarity in the Shire.

But as Tolkien notes, in addition to their wealth 'Bilbo and Frodo Baggins were as bachelors very exceptional, as they were also in many other ways, such as their friendship with Elves.' The nephew of 'mad Baggins,' as he eventually became known, Frodo was something of an aesthete and intellectual, who, 'to the amazement of sensible folk . . . was sometimes seen far from home walking in the hills and woods under the starlight.'[4] None of this was usual among their peers, and Sam the gardener, although recently and exceptionally lettered, was a more typical hobbit than his fellow Companions—or as Tolkien put it, 'the genuine hobbit.'

Like some readers, Tolkien himself sometimes found Sam, as he wrote:

> very 'trying.' He is a more representative hobbit than any others that we have to see much of; and he has consequently a stronger ingredient of that quality which even some hobbits found at times hard to bear: a vulgarity—by which I do not mean a mere 'down-to-earthiness'—a mental myopia which is proud of itself, a smugness (in varying degrees) and cocksureness, and a readiness to measure and sum up all things from a limited experience, largely enshrined in sententious traditional 'wisdom.' . . . Imagine Sam without his education by Bilbo and his fascination with things Elvish![5]

Even with this kind of conservative peer pressure, however, your behaviour had to be extreme to land you in any real trouble, for the Shire at this time had hardly any government: 'Families for the most part managed their own affairs. . . . The only real official in the Shire at this date was

the Mayor of Michel Delving,' and 'almost his only duty was
to preside at banquets. . . .' Otherwise there were only heredi-
tary heads of clans, plus a Postmaster and First Shirriff—the
latter less for Inside Work than 'to see that Outsiders of any
kind, great or small, did not make themselves a nuisance.'[6]

ENGLISHNESS

Now it doesn't take any great perceptiveness to see in 'these
charming, absurd, helpless' (and not-so-helpless) hobbits a
self-portrait of the English, something which Tolkien admitted: '"The Shire" is based on rural England and not any
other country in the world,' and more specifically the West
Midlands: Hobbiton 'is in fact more or less a Warwickshire
village of about the period of the Diamond Jubilee' (i.e.
1897).[7]

Compare the portrait by George Orwell writing in 1940,
and one still instantly recognizable, albeit sadly altered in
some respects, of a conservative people neither artistically
nor intellectually inclined, though with 'a certain power of
acting without thought'; taciturn, preferring tacit under-
standings to formal explication; endowed with a love of
flowers and animals, valuing privateness and the liberty of
the individual, and respecting constitutionalism and legal-
ity; not puritanical and without definite religious belief, but
strangely gentle (and this has changed most, especially during the 1980s), with a hatred of war and militarism that co-
exists with a strong unconscious patriotism. Orwell summed
up English society as 'a strange mixture of reality and illu-
sion, democracy and privilege, humbug and decency.'[8]

True, these attributes are inextricably mingled with ones
that the English have wanted to find in the mirror; nor are
they eternal and immutable. Because this image partakes of
a national pastoral fantasy, however, it does not follow that
it has no reality. A social or literary criticism that is afraid to
admit the relative truth of clichés and stereotypes is ham-
strung from the start. Also, it is worth noting that Tolkien's
portrait is not altogether a flattering one; it includes greed,
small-minded parochialism and philistinism, at least—even
in Frodo, Sam and the other hobbits of his story were able to
rise above these regrettable characteristics of the English
bourgeoisie.

However, although Tolkien drew on the tiny corner of the
world that is the West Midlands of England, readers from

virtually everywhere else in the world connect the hobbits
with a rustic people of their own, relatively untouched by
modernity—if not still actually existing, then from the alternative reality of folk- and fairy-tale. Doubtless this has been
made possible by setting his books in a place that, while it
feels like N.W. Europe, is made strange and wonderful by its
imaginary time. Otherwise, I have no doubt, they would have
suffered from the same limitations of time and place as
Kipling's *Puck of Pook's Hill* and G.K. Chesterton's poems,
however wonderful these otherwise may be. Tolkien's tale,
in contrast, has probably achieved as close to universality as
is given to art.

COUNTRY FOLK

The hobbits are recognizably modern in important respects,
especially in their bourgeois and anti-heroic tenor. Thus,
one famous hobbit, when asked by a large eagle, 'What is
finer than flying?,' only allowed his native tact, and caution,
to overrule suggesting 'A warm bath and late breakfast on
the lawn afterwards.'[9] As several commentators have noticed, it is crucial that Bilbo and Frodo *be* modern, in order
to 'accommodate modernity without surrendering to it,'[10] by
mediating between ourselves and the ancient and foreign
world they inhabit. But in other ways, the hobbits have much
older roots. They remind us of 'the archetypal pre-Industrial
Revolution English yeoman with simple needs, simple goals,
and a common-sense approach to life,'[11] and also of the English before their defeat in 1066, when the 'Norman Yoke'
imposed centralized autocratic government, a foreign language and an alien cultural tradition.

The bucolic hobbits also clearly fall within the long tradition in English letters of nostalgic pastoralism, celebrating a
time 'when there was less noise and more green.'[12] As Martin J. Weiner notes, 'Idealization of the countryside has a
long history in Britain.' It extends from Tennyson's mid-
Victorian *English Idylls* and William Morris's 'fair green garden of Northern Europe,' through the rural essays of Richard
Jefferies and the Poet Laureate Alfred Austin's *Haunts of Ancient Peace* (1902)—which could easily be the title of a song
by Van Morrison today—to Kipling's 'Our England is a garden,' and George Sturt listening to his gardener (note), 'in
whose quiet voice,' he felt, 'I am privileged to hear the natural fluent, unconscious talk, as it goes on over the face of the

country, of the English race.' In short, a deep cultural gulf had opened between England's southern and rural 'green and pleasant land' and her northern and industrial 'dark satanic mills'; or as Weiner puts it, with unintentional aptness, 'The power of the machine was invading and blighting the Shire.'[13]

The irony is, of course, that since 1851 over half the population on this island has lived in towns, and by then England was already the world's first urban nation. Thus, as Weiner writes, 'The less practically important rural England became, the more easily could it come to stand simply for an alternative and complementary set of values, a psychic balance wheel.'[14] But few things are that simple, and when applied to Tolkien, such glib simplification has led to a great deal of misunderstanding. The related charges commonly laid at Tolkien's door are several, and severe. They are also almost entirely mistaken, so I shall use them to arrive at the truth of the matter.

NATION AND CLASS

One of the first critics to attack Tolkien was Catharine Stimpson, in 1969. 'An incorrigible nationalist,' she wrote, Tolkien 'celebrates the English bourgeois pastoral idyll. Its characters, tranquil and well fed, live best in placid, philistine, provincial rural cosiness.'[15]

Now it is true that the hobbits (excepting Bilbo and Frodo, and perhaps Sam . . . and Merry and Pippin) would indeed have preferred to live quiet rural lives, if they could have. Unfortunately for them, and Stimpson's point, there is much more to Middle-earth than the Shire. By the same token, any degree of English nationalism that the hobbits represent is highly qualified. Tolkien himself pointed out that 'hobbits are not a Utopian vision, or recommended as an ideal in their own or any age. They, as all peoples and their situations, are an historical accident—as the Elves point out to Frodo—and an impermanent one in the long view.'[16] It is also possible, as Jonathan Bate suggests, to draw a distinction between love of the local land, on the one hand, and patriotic love of the fatherland on the other. In *The Lord of the Rings*, the lovingly detailed specificities of the natural world—which include but far outrun those of the Shire—far exceed any kind of abstract nationalism.[17]

Stimpson also accuses Tolkien of 'class snobbery'[18]—that

is, the lord of the manor's disdain for commoners, and, by extension, the working class. Well, in *The Hobbit*, perhaps; but only zealous detectors of orcism and trollism would ignore its other virtues, such as any quality as a story. And its hero, if no peasant, is plainly no lord. But with *The Lord of the Rings*—if this charge means anything worse than a sort of chivalrous paternalism, appropriate to someone growing up at the turn of this century, which now looks dated—then it fails.

There is certainly class awareness. But the idioms of Tolkien's various hobbits only correspond to their social classes in the same way as do those of contemporary humans. The accent and idiom of Sam (arguably the real hero of the book) and most other hobbits are those of a rural peasantry, while those of Frodo, Bilbo and their close friends range through the middle classes. Or take Orcs; their distinguishing characteristics are a love of machines and loud noises (especially explosions), waste, vandalism and destruction for its own sake; also, they alone torture and kill for fun. Their language, accordingly, is 'at all times full of hate and anger,' and composed of 'brutal jargons, scarcely sufficient even for their own needs, unless it were for curses and abuse.' In the Third Age, 'Orcs and Trolls spoke as they would, without love of words or things; and their language was actually more degraded and filthy,' writes Tolkien, 'than I have shown it.' As he adds, too truly, 'Much the same sort of talk can still be heard among the orc-minded; dreary and repetitive with hatred and contempt. . . .'[19]

But Orc speech is not all the same; there are at least three kinds, and none are necessarily 'working-class.'[20] And it can be found today among members of any social class; nor is money a bar. In fact, virtually all of Tolkien's major villains—Smaug, Saruman, the Lord of the Nazgûl, and presumably Sauron too—speak in unmistakably posh tones.[21] After all, the orc-minded are mere servants of Mordor; its contemporary masters (or rather, master-servants) much more resemble the Nazgûl, although today they probably wear expensive suits and ride private jets rather than quasi-pterodactyls. And although many fewer than Orcs (who knows? perhaps there are exactly nine[22]), they are infinitely more powerful, and to be feared.

There is also the obvious and fundamental fact of *The Lord of the Rings* as a tale of 'the hour of the Shire-folk, when they arise from their quiet fields to shake the towers and counsels of the Great.'[23] Nonetheless, the charge of pandering to social hierarchy has proved durable. Another unpleasant and related accusation sometimes made is racism.[24] Now it is true that Tolkien's evil creatures are frequently 'swart, slant-eyed,' and tend to come from the south ('the cruel Haradrim') and east ('the wild Easterlings')[25]—both threatening directions in Tolkien's 'moral cartography.'[26] It is also true that black—as in Breath, Riders, Hand, Years, Land, Speech—is often a terrible colour, especially when contrasted with Gandalf the White, the White Rider, and so on. But the primary association of black here is with night and darkness, not race. And there are counter-examples: Saruman's sign is a white hand; Aragorn's standard is mostly black; the Black Riders were not actually black, except their outer robes; and the Black Stone of Erech is connected with Aragorn's forebear, Isildur.[27]

Overall, Tolkien is drawing on centuries of such moral valuation, not unrelated to historical experience attached to his chosen setting in order to convey something immediately recognizable in the context of his story. As Kathleen Herbert noticed, Orcs sound very like the first horrified reports in Europe of the invading Huns in the fourth and fifth centuries: 'broad-shouldered, bow-legged, devilishly effective fighters, moving fast, talking a language that sounds like no human speech (probably Turkic) and practising ghastly tortures with great relish.'[28] (Théoden may well have been modelled on Theodoric I, the aged Visigothic king who died leading his warriors in a charge against Attila's Huns in the Battle of Chalons.)

Perhaps the worst you could say is that Tolkien doesn't actually go out of his way to forestall the possibility of a racist interpretation. (I say 'possibility' because it is ridiculous to assume that readers automatically transfer their feelings about Orcs to all the swart or slant-eyed people they encounter in the street.) But as Virginia Luling has pointed out, the appearance of racism is deceptive, 'not only because Tolkien in his non-fictional writing several times repudiated racist ideas, but because . . . in his sub-creation the whole intellectual underpinning of racism is absent.'[29] In any case, such an interpretation as the story in *The Lord of the Rings* proceeds, that would get increasingly harder to maintain— and this relates to another common criticism, also voiced by

Stimpson, that Tolkien's characters divide neatly into 'good and evil, nice and nasty.'[30] But as anyone who has really read it could tell you, the initial semi-tribal apportioning of moral probity increasingly breaks down, as evil emerges 'among the kingly Gondorians, the blond Riders of Rohan, the seemingly incorruptible wizards, and even the thoroughly English hobbit-folk of the Shire.'[31] (Incidentally, hobbits appear to be brown-skinned, not white.[32]) By the same token, Frodo, Gollum, Boromir and Denethor all experience intense inner struggles over what the right thing to do is, with widely varying outcomes; and as Le Guin has noted, several major characters have a 'shadow.'[33] In Frodo's case, there are arguably two: Sam and Gollum, who is himself doubled as Gollum/Stinker and Sméagol/Slinker, as Sam calls him.

'If you want to write a tale of this sort,' Tolkien once wrote, 'you must consult your roots, and a man of the North-west of the Old World will set his heart and the action of his tale in an imaginary world of that air, and that situation: with the Shoreless Sea of his innumerable ancestors to the West, and the endless lands (out of which enemies mostly come) to the East.'[34]

Thus, as Clyde Kilby recounts, when Tolkien was asked what lay east and south of Middle-earth, he replied: '"Rhûn is the Elvish word for east. Asia, China, Japan, and all the things which people in the West regard as far away. And south of Harad is Africa, the hot countries." Then Mr. Resnick asked, "That makes Middle-earth Europe, doesn't it?" To which Tolkien replied, "Yes, of course—Northwestern Europe . . . where my imagination comes from".' (In which case, as Tolkien also agreed, Mordor 'would be roughly in the Balkans.')[35]

He reacted sharply to reading a description of Middle-earth as 'Nordic,' however: 'Not *Nordic*, please! A word I personally dislike; it is associated, though of French origin, with racialist theories. . . .' He also contested Auden's assertion that for him 'the North is a sacred direction': 'That is not true. The North-west of Europe, where I (and most of my ancestors) have lived, has my affection, as a man's home should. I love its atmosphere, and know more of its histories and languages than I do of other parts; but it is not "sacred," nor does it exhaust my affections.'[36]

It is also striking that the races in Middle-earth are most striking in their variety and autonomy. I suppose that this

could be seen as an unhealthy emphasis on 'race'; it seems
to me rather an assertion of the wonder of multicultural difference. And given that most of Middle-earth's peoples are
closely tried to a particular geography and ecology, and
manage to live there without exploiting it to the point of destruction, isn't this what is nowadays called bioregionalism?
But no kind of apartheid is involved: one of the subplots of
The Lord of the Rings concerns an enduring friendship between members of races traditionally estranged (Gimli and
Legolas), and the most important union in the book, between Aragorn and Arwen, is an 'interracial' marriage. As
usual, the picture is a great deal more complex than the critics, although not necessarily the public, seem to see.

NOTES

1. Hubert Butler, *Escape from the Anthill* (Mullingar: The
   Lilliput Press, 1986), 95.
2. J.R.R. Tolkien, *The Hobbit* (London: Grafton Books, 1991),
   15. (Henceforth *Hobbit;* all page numbers are from this edition.) J.R.R. Tolkien, *The Lord of the Rings* (London:
   Grafton Books, 1991), I, 17, 18. (Henceforth *LoR;* all page
   numers are from this edition.) *Hobbit,* 16; *LoR,* I, 23. 'Anglo-hobbitic': T.A. Shippey, *The Road to Middle-Earth*
   (London: George Allen & Unwin, 1992 [1982]), 91.
3. Hobbits: *LoR,* I, 59; III, 173; II, 202; I, 50, 26, 219.
4. Frodo: *LoR,* I, 25, 67.
5. Sam: Humphrey Carpenter (ed.), *The Letters of J.R.R.
   Tolkien* (London: George Allen & Unwin, 1981), 105, 329
   (on Sam). (Henceforth *Letters,* with page rather than letter numbers given.)
6. Shire: *LoR,* I, 28, 29, 75.
7. Shire/rural England: *Letters,* 250, 230; and see Clyde
   Kilby, *Tolkien and the Silmarillion* (Berkhamsted: Lion
   Publishing, 1977), 51. The hobbits' obsession with family
   genealogy is an Icelandic touch, however.
8. George Orwell, 'The Lion and the Unicorn: Socialism and
   the English Genius,' 527–64 in *Collected Essays, Journalism
   and Letters* (London: Secker and Warburg, 1968).
9. Warm bath: *Hobbit,* 113.
10. 'Accommodate modernity': Hugh Brogan, 'Tolkien's
    Great War,' in Gillian Avery and Julia Briggs (eds.), *Chil-
    dren and Thier Books* (Oxford, Eng.: Clarendon, 1989),
    360. *Cf.* Shippey, *Road,* 55.

11. 'English yeoman': David Harvey, *The Song of Middle-Earth: J.R.R. Tolkien's Themes, Symbols and Myths* (London: George Allen & Unwin, 1985), 114.

12. Less noise: *Hobbit*, 15.

13. Martin J. Weiner, *English Culture and the Decline of the Industrial Spirit 1850–1980* (London: Penguin, 1985), 47, 61 (Sturt), 81, and Chapter 4 generally. See also Alun Howkins, 'The Discovery of Rural England,' 62–88 in Robert Coll and Philip Dodd (eds.), *Englishness. Politics and Culture 1880–1920* (London: Croon Helm, 1986).

14. Weiner, *English Culture*, 47, 49.

15. Catharine R. Stimpson, *J.R.R. Tolkien* (New York: Columbia University Press, 1969) (Columbia Essays on Modern Writers No. 41), 8, 13. See Hal Colebatch's critique of Stimpson in his *Return of the Heroes: The Lord of the Rings, Star Wars and Contemporary Culture* (Perth: Australian Institute for Public Policy, 1990), 61–66.

16. Historical accident: *Letters*, 197.

17. Land/fatherland: Jonathan Bate, *Romantic Ecology: Wordsworth and the Environmental Tradition* (London: Routledge, 1991), 11.

18. Stimpson, *Tolkien*, 13.

19. Orcs: *LoR*, II, 54; III, 520, 524.

20. 'Working-class': Brian Rosebury, *Tolkien: A Critical Assessment* (London: St. Martin's, 1992), 75–76.

21. Posh Tones: the last point is made by Colebatch, *Return*, 64.

22. Exactly nine modern Ringwraiths: joke.

23. Hour of the Shire-folk: *LoR*, I, 354.

24. Accusation: for a recent and typically thoughtless repetition, see Roz Kaveney, 'The Ring recycled,' *New Statesman & Society* (20/27.12.91) 47, who also associates Tolkien with 'a broadside attack on modernism and even on realism' (is *nothing* sacred?), and anachronistically blames him for current 'American commercial fantasy and science fiction.'

25. Evil creatures: *LoR*, II, 14, 357.

26. 'Moral cartography': Walter Scheps, 'The Fairy-tale Morality of *The Lord of the Rings*,' in Jared Lobdell (ed.), *A Tolkien Compass* (La Salle, IL: Open Court, 1975), 44–45; also 46, for discussion of the instances of blackness.

27. Counter-examples: see Rosebury, *Tolkien*, 79.

28. Kathleen Herbert, *Spellcraft: Old English Heroic Legends* (Hockwold-cum-Wilton, Norfolk: Anglo-Saxon Books, 1993) 271, 225.
29. Virginia Luling, 'An Anthropologist in Middle-Earth,' in Patricia Reynolds and Glen H. GoodKnight (eds.), *Proceedings of the J.R.R. Tolkien Centenary Conference* (Milton Keynes: The Tolkien Society, and Altadena, CA: Mythopoeic Press, 1995). However, as she adds, the Orcs—as distinct from the Haradrim, Variags and Easterlings—'are a separate problem, and one that Tolkien himself never really solved' (p. 56); see J.R.R. Tolkien, *Morgoth's Ring*, ed. Christopher Tolkien (London: HarperCollins, 1994), for his efforts to do so.
30. Stimpson, *Tolkien*, 18.
31. 'Kingly Gondorians': Brian Attebery, *Strategies of Fantasy* (Bloomington: University of Indiana, 1992), 33.
32. Brown-skinned: *LoR*, III, 229.
33. Ursula K. Le Guin, *The Language of the Night; Essays on Fantasy and Science Fiction*, ed. Susan Wood (London: The Women's Press, 1989), 57–58; and see Attebery, *Strategies*, 33, and Rosebury, *Tolkien*, 75–76. (This is simplistic?)
34. A tale of this sort: *Letters*, 212.
35. Kilby, *Tolkien*, 51–52.
36. North-west Europe: *Letters*, 375–76.

Care for the Earth and for Each Other

Robley Evans

Tolkien argues that there is much of value in Western society that should be saved, writes Robley
Evans. In presenting a mythic story that invites readers to learn to respect all living things, Tolkien gives
emotional and spiritual meaning to the "facts" of the
Primary World—the physical world that often seems
bleak. Evans is author of the *Writers for the Seventies*
book on Tolkien, from which this essay is excerpted.

If we compare Tolkien to other contemporary writers, we see
major differences. Unlike such writers of fantasy as Kurt Von-
negut, Tolkien is never crudely satiric; gentleness and love
pervade his work and soften the criticism of modern society
implicit in it. Where other authors present a bleak picture of
the wasteland in which the soul struggles to survive alone,
Tolkien gives us the Fellowship of the Ring as a happier alternative, a small society of loving creatures who are not alone in
the universe. Tolkien argues that there is much of value in
Western culture which should be saved, which *will* be saved,
by the imaginative beings who have power to believe in themselves. Tolkien is a conservative in this sense; for all the elements of the fantastic in his work, the preservation of traditional values is most important to him. The fantastic affirms
those values rather than attempting to substitute something
else for them. Tolkien's writing style, too, is not meant to sur-
prise or shock us; it is always subordinate to the story being
told. It is his retelling of our most deeply believed myths about
ourselves that makes *The Lord of the Rings* so moving.

WORDS SHARE THE REALITY OF THE PRIMARY WORLD

Tolkien is read because he tells a good story; his power to command Secondary Belief in his readers is real. History comes

alive in the characters and events of *The Lord of the Rings* because Tolkien creates speeches and actions which have the "inner consistency of reality" and are not absolutely and destructively rooted in the "observed fact" of the Primary World. He has chosen to tell a story, rather, than write a philosophic discourse, and this decision was important because a narrative presents "inner" reality in a way a discursive essay does not: imagined beings who take their life from the hands of their creator touch our emotions, our imaginations, our religious sense of wonder, in ways words addressed to the intellect alone cannot. As William Blake wrote long ago, we cannot really imagine God as a cloud; we must imagine Him in the form most meaningful to us, that of a man. Men, or created beings of other races, act enough like men in Tolkien's fantasies, to remind us that we, too, progress through time toward death; that we, too, love life and fear evil. And in this way the fantastic in its narrative form comes closer to representing that total body of knowledge and being which is ourself more than many other literary kinds. In order to make this happen, the fantasist gives us actions and shapes which seem familiar; but he also frees us from dependency upon "observed fact" so that the imagination can work and our vision of the unknown world can show us new things in ourselves.

Behind Tolkien's choice of form lies an assumption about the nature of man which shines through his work: that men can love, admire good deeds, can seek truth because it is good. They are not "bad"; they are imperceptive, they are weak insofar as excessive self-pride makes them misuse their particular powers; they are available, however, to correction, to change, to the Power, used only for good, of the Enchanter. Words and literary forms are not things apart from human beings. They come up from the body and the feelings attached to the Primary World, as they are, and they share in that reality. And much more. The "Joy" of which Tolkien writes in "On Fairy-Stories" is "heavenly" all right, but it underlies the events in *The Lord of the Rings*, too, in the "turn" of the happy ending, and in the life of the narration itself.

A MYTHIC STORY IN WHICH ALL CAN SHARE

This is important because we also read Tolkien for other reasons which come through to us because of his way of presenting them. Tolkien has gone against the present style of literary fashion; he does not give us the private rhetoric of the symbolist or the inner-directed world of the despairing self-analyst whose psychological conflicts spin out a novel's length. Rather than make a meaningful world out of an individual's isolated and particular nature, he returns to the myths of the past and to the mythic story of the Quest in which all men can share. This argues for the universal significance of experience and so for the pervasive moral effects of the imagination. Individual suffering and bewilderment reveal valuable meaning in a mythic context; nor is suffering exceptional and meaningful only to the individual. If as Mark Schorer says, myths are images "that give philosophical meaning to the facts of ordinary life," then a writer of myth writes for his whole society as well as every individual who suffers and imagines in it. Fantasy is not escape in the sense of flight from reality, Tolkien reminds us, but an affirmation of man's ability to order reality, a schema for handling the problems which power creates, for "realizing imagined wonder." His success at reconstituting the fairy-story for the twentieth century lies in part in his sense of our moral necessities.

Another reason for reading Tolkien is his assertion that the Imagination has value in the Primary World. For many people, growing up in a culture which seems to emphasize the uniformity of lives on the assembly line or in split-level suburbs, works of fantasy must be suspect because they represent imagined existence and exceptional beings. Tolkien shows throughout *The Hobbit* and *The Lord of the Rings* that we can be surprised by our fellows: the hobbits of the Shire perform heroic feats we would never have expected. But it is this unexpected quality of the imagination, popping up when least expected, that readers must find attractive, especially since this power for good solves problems, directs actions, opens up possibilities in Tolkien's fantasies. And for readers who resist the homogeneity and conformity of contemporary life, there is appeal in the variety of imagined beings—elves, dwarves, ents, hobbits—who appear in the hills and valleys of Middle-earth. Not only the profusion of races, but the respect which they can show to each other must be important for Americans perplexed by racial segregation, sexual discrimination, xenophobia and their divisive, hate-engendering effects. In *The Lord of the Rings*, we find a Fellowship, a United Nations, based upon common needs and shared affection, even between the most disparate peoples. The fight against "possessiveness," the possibilities of "Recovery," are happy alternatives in a possessive society.

RESPECT FOR ALL LIVING THINGS

In Tolkien's world, respect is paid not only to other "races" but to living things generally. Perhaps the most important problem in the latter half of the twentieth century is presented by the natural environment, ravaged by possessive men in search of wealth and power. In the Trilogy, the evil beings are connected with such desecration; Saruman and Sauron both attack the natural organic world, leveling forests, covering vegetation with ash-piles, factories and their waste, the "produce" of slave-worked mines. But those who fight against evil respect the natural world, as guardians of all created beings. The ents care for their trees, the dwarves for their gleaming minerals. Aragorn finds help for wounds in the *athelas*, a wild herb. Sam grows an elven tree, the *Mallorn*, far from its home in Lorien. The imagination requires that even plants be permitted their own natures, and shown care rather than possessiveness. This general respect for all created life in *The Lord of the Rings* speaks to those among us who fear the disappearance of redwoods and whales, mountain wilderness and hidden seashores to serve society's destructive needs. If we try to turn every mountain valley into a national park with camping areas, general stores and play grounds, we have remade it in our image, and so extended a step further "the drab blur of triteness or familiarity" which must ultimately threaten our own necessary sense of wonder at other forms of life. And under our heavy hand, such unique life can be extinguished. *Care for the world* might be the theme of Tolkien's Trilogy.

Nor does the Imagination deny the existence of evil. Our society can be accused of hiding reality under its images: the glossy prints of the large-circulation magazines or the smiling caricatures of housewives discovering a new soap in television commercials. Distress is smoothed away, and suffering denied not only existence but value. People hurt, however; they suffer from poverty, hunger, loneliness, fear and a long list of human symptoms which no soap product or movie star can cure. They also suffer from the absence of great causes for which to suffer, paradoxical as that may seem. In Tolkien's fantasy, we do not escape from evil: there is no running away from the Shadow of Sauron. The ways in which created beings respond to the challenge such power presents distinguish them; make them more complex in nature than we think at first; make them moral. For a reader tired of seeing human beings as only partial figures caught in the conventions of social life and prescribed rituals, the revelation of hidden natures available for good or evil is valuable.

AN EMPHASIS ON FEELING, RATHER THAN REASON

And, finally, beyond it social implications, the imagination in its guise of the fantastic, separate from "observed fact," gives life to the world in a way the sciences, the academic disciplines which emphasize reason or mathematical formulae, do not. As man begins to discover more and more about the laws which govern life, and seems to be reducing life to equations tested in a laboratory, our human response is to seek the unreasonable, the irrational, feelings and visions which may be condemned by the scientist because they cannot be analyzed or represented statistically. Love, responsibility, and will power cannot be computed, yet they exist, and seem to have much more to do with human conduct than laws and figures. The appeal of fantasy implies instinctive rejection of what seems impersonal, unfeeling, insensitive to our human desires, in the century of nuclear bombs, germ warfare, and government policy beyond the power of any individual to influence.

In fact, Tolkien emphasizes feeling in *The Lord of the Rings.* Characters not only develop love for one another, they express it in companionship, in sacrifice, in loyalty. They show it by kissing and holding hands. They respond to their feelings by expressing anger or love. They have strong responses to events, and make decisions based on such feelings. Suffering, looked upon as an evil in a society which does not have a religious context in which to understand and accept it, is feeling which draws characters together in Tolkien and alters their vision of the world and of themselves. To confront anguish or pain in life—rather than repressing it and denying its existence—is a step toward reality.

THE INDIVIDUAL'S ABILITY TO MAKE THINGS HAPPEN

But the value of strong feeling as a causal element speaks to another point in Tolkien's work: the emphasis upon the individual and his ability to *do* something, to make things happen, even against what seem enormous odds. Part of the boredom which men experience in modern society comes from feeling that there is nothing worthwhile they can do to express themselves as individuals. After a day at the office, shuffling papers, we turn to expensive cars, drink or casual sex to give us a sense of purpose and value which the ordinary round of life does not provide. But these interests are not enough to really satisfy that wish to be "meaningful" which commitment to a larger social or spiritual purpose can give. In Tolkien's fantasy, we can see that under imaginative direction, action is possible. Men and hobbits make decisions and then take steps to fulfill them. Feeling and ideas are not bottled up and finally reduced to dreams, but lead to changes, realizations of vision, which imaginative created beings may direct. The quests of Frodo and Aragorn are a series of events in which the Hero chooses and performs.

Not that all actions have to be glorious. Part of the sympathy we feel for Frodo and Sam, who "act" heroically in their journey through Mordor, may come from our sense that to endure and be patient is all we can do. Frodo's heroism does not lie in his warrior's abilities (which are small) or his command of men. It lies in his commitment to a greater vision of life than himself, and it is his dogged plodding through the dispiriting wastes that makes him so significant. The justification for his heroism lies in the larger purposes he fulfills as Ring-bearer. We sympathize with his loneliness, his desperation, but we see he completes the designs of a universal plan, indeed, is the most important element in that plan. We may feel no such plan exists for us, but neither was Frodo very sure; his persistence in his quest is made in spite of, perhaps because of, this uncertainty, a willed affirmation of his own value. Frodo *puts* value in the universe, through his own efforts, and it is in this heroic act that we may find the positive analogy for our lives in the Primary World.

SOCIETY IS WORTH SAVING

We should also remember that Frodo's self-sacrifice is not only for the defeat of evil; it is also for the good of society, for the whole Community of created beings. This suggests, in turn, that in the mind of the fantasist, society is worth saving. It is not a mechanical horror designed to grind the individual down. Instead, personal commitment—*service*—is honored by the citizens of Middle-earth. The individual finds a responsible place for himself in his society; those who live outside society are identified with tyranny and self-destruction. A major reason for Tolkien's popularity among students and the "rebellious young" may be his classic insistence that the individual finds true freedom in the service of good, and that good can be social, providing security and purpose for others without being destructive of singularity and wilfullness.

Behind Tolkien's work, in other words, we can find a deeply religious commitment to Western culture and its values, ragged and unsatisfactory as they may seem to some of us. But Tolkien's use, in his major work, of our most pervasive myths—the Quest, the sacrifice of the god for the renewal of life, the battle of good and evil—suggests that he does not feel we have come so far from our origins that art and life, fantasy and human needs, are far apart. That he chose to cast his story in the Middle-earth of an earlier age, with a set of characters whom we may or may not have met before, argues for his faith in our imagination and our ability to believe. We must be able to want to realize "imagined wonder" in spite of the Primary World in which we also live. That we read *The Lord of the Rings* with tears and love argues for his success: we are willing to believe in this form of the myth of our life. Like the Christian myth which underlies Tolkien's view of experience in the twentieth century, the myth of the War of the Ring gives emotional and spiritual meaning to much of what we know. It, too, affirms the grandest moral purposes of the universe, and asserts that there are ultimate values in which we may believe. As Thomas Carlyle put it almost one hundred and fifty years ago, in a century when values seemed as problematic as in this one: "The Universe is not dead and demoniacal, a charnel-house with spectres; but godlike, and my Father's!"[1] Belief is not just faith in a church doctrine; it is a commitment to a meaningful reality and to our ability to believe in ourself. For *The Lord of the Rings* is a "joyful" book; and its happy ending is not the only source of that knowledge. We read it with delight because it makes us feel that pleasure, and thus it tells us not only that the universe is godlike but that we are, too. Tolkien can be accused of sentimentality, but this is not always a pejorative epithet. Feeling which reunites lovers, discovers lost children or parents, returns the wanderer to his long-abandoned home—feeling has an honorable place in the structure of the imagination, and our response to Tolkien's myth is an honest guide to our own—and society's—reality.

1. Thomas Carlyle, "The Everlasting Yea," *Sartor Resartus* (New York: Doubleday, Doran & Co., 1937), p. 188.

CHAPTER 3

The Writer's Art: Style and Sources in *The Lord of the Rings*

READINGS ON
J.R.R. TOLKIEN

The Lord of the Rings Succeeds on a Mythic Scale

W.H. Auden

Renowned poet and author W.H. Auden celebrated the publication of the third volume of *The Lord of the Rings* trilogy with the following essay. Auden writes that it is difficult to present a clear-cut conflict between Good and Evil and a story of a heroic Quest in a way that seems relevant to real life: an impersonal narrative seems just a document, while a subjective tale about a hero's quest seems to have little to do with the lives of whose who cannot take such journeys. Tolkien has managed to combine quest and conflict, says Auden, while maintaining a sense of historical and social reality with an attention to detail matched by no previous writer.

In *The Return of the King*, Frodo Baggins fulfills his Quest, the realm of Sauron is ended forever, the Third Age is over and J.R.R. Tolkien's trilogy *The Lord of the Rings* complete. I rarely remember a book about which I have had such violent arguments. Nobody *seems* to have a moderate opinion: either, like myself, people find it a masterpiece of its genre or they cannot abide it, and among the hostile there are some, I must confess, for whose literary judgment I have great respect. A few of these may have been put off by the first forty pages of the first chapter of the first volume in which the daily life of the hobbits is described; this is light comedy and light comedy is not Mr. Tolkien's forte. In most cases, however, the objection must go far deeper. I can only suppose that some people object to Heroic Quests and Imaginary Worlds on principle; such, they feel, cannot be anything but light "escapist" reading. That a man like Mr.

Reprinted from W.H. Auden, "At the End of the Quest, Victory," *The New York Times*, January 22, 1956, by permission. Copyright © 1956 by The New York Times.

Tolkien, the English philologist who teaches at Oxford, should lavish such incredible pains upon a genre which is, for them, trifling by definition, is, therefore, very shocking.

The difficulty of presenting a complete picture of reality lies in the gulf between the subjectively real, a man's experience of his own existence, and the objectively real, his experience of the lives of others and the world about him. Life, as I experience it in my own person, is primarily a continuous succession of choices between alternatives, made for a short-term or long-term purpose; the actions I take, that is to say, are less significant to me than the conflicts of motives, temptations, doubts in which they originate. Further, my subjective experience of time is not of a cyclical motion outside myself but of an irreversible history of unique moments which are made by my decisions.

False Image vs. Impersonal Document

For objectifying this experience, the natural image is that of a journey with a purpose, beset by dangerous hazards and obstacles, some merely difficult, others actively hostile. But when I observe my fellow men, such an image seems false. I can see, for example, that only the rich and those on vacation can take journeys; most men, most of the time must work in one place.

I cannot observe them making choices, only the actions they take and, if I know someone well, I can usually predict correctly how he will act in a given situation. I observe, all too often, men in conflict with each other, wars and hatreds, but seldom, if ever, a clear-cut issue between Good on the one side and Evil on the other, though I also observe that both sides usually describe it as such. If, then, I try to describe what I see as if I were an impersonal camera, I shall produce, not a Quest, but a "naturalistic" document.

Both extremes, of course, falsify life. There are medieval Quests which deserve the criticism made by Erich Auerbach in his book *Mimesis:*

> The world of knightly proving is a world of adventure. It not only contains a practically uninterrupted series of adventures; more specifically, it contains nothing but the requisites of adventure * * * Except feats of arms and love, nothing occurs in the courtly world—and even these two are of a special sort: they are not occurrences or emotions which can be absent for a time; they are permanently connected with the person of the perfect knight, they are part of his definition, so

that he cannot for one moment be without adventure in arms nor for one moment without amorous entanglement * * * His exploits are feats of arms, not 'war,' for they are feats accomplished at random which do not fit into any politically purposive pattern.

And there are contemporary "thrillers" in which the identification of hero and villain with contemporary politics is depressingly obvious. On the other hand, there are naturalistic novels in which the characters are the mere puppets of Fate, or rather of the author, who, from some mysterious point of freedom, contemplates the workings of Fate.

TOLKIEN COMBINES THE HEROIC QUEST WITH A SENSE OF REALITY

If, as I believe, Mr. Tolkien has succeeded more completely than any previous writer in this genre in using the traditional properties of the Quest, the heroic journey, the Numinous Object, the conflict between Good and Evil while at the same time satisfying our sense of historical and social reality, it should be possible to show how he has succeeded. To begin with, no previous writer has, to my knowledge, created an imaginary world and a feigned history in such detail. By the time the reader has finished the trilogy, including the appendices to this last volume, he knows as much about Mr. Tolkien's Middle-earth, its landscape, its fauna and flora, its peoples, their languages, their history, their cultural habits, as, outside his special field, he knows about the actual world.

Mr. Tolkien's world may not be the same as our own: it includes, for example, elves, beings who know good and evil but have not fallen, and, though not physically indestructible, do not suffer natural death. It is afflicted by Sauron, an incarnation of absolute evil, and creatures like Shelob, the monster spider, or the orcs who are corrupt past hope of redemption. But it is a world of intelligible law, not mere wish; the reader's sense of the credible is never violated.

Even the One Ring, the absolute physical and psychological weapon which must corrupt any who dares to use it, is a perfectly plausible hypothesis from which the political duty to destroy it which motivates Frodo's Quest logically follows.

A TICKLISH BUSINESS

To present the conflict between Good and Evil as a war in which the good side is ultimately victorious is a ticklish

---

ELEMENTS OF A QUEST STORY

In an essay on "The Quest Hero," W.H. Auden spells out six essential elements of a typical Quest tale.

1) A precious Object and/or Person to be found and possessed or married.

2) A long journey to find it, for its whereabouts are not originally known to the seekers.

3) A hero. The precious Object cannot be found by anybody, but only by the one person who possesses the right qualities of breeding or character.

4) A test or series of Tests by which the unworthy are screened out, and the hero revealed.

5) The Guardians of the Object who must be overcome before it can be won. They may be simply a further test of the hero's *arete*, or they may be malignant in themselves.

6) The Helpers who with their knowledge and magical powers assist the hero and but for whom he would never succeed. They may appear in human or in animal form.

W.H. Auden, "The Quest Hero," *Texas Quarterly* IV (1962). Reprinted in Neil D. Isaacs and Rose A. Zimbardo, eds., *Tolkien and the Critics: Essays on J.R.R. Tolkien's* The Lord of the Rings. Notre Dame, IN: University of Notre Dame, 1968.

---

business. Our historical experience tells us that physical power and, to a large extent, mental power are morally neutral and effectively real: wars are won by the stronger side, just or unjust. At the same time most of us believe that the essence of the Good is love and freedom so that Good cannot impose itself by force without ceasing to be good.

The battles in the Apocalypse and *Paradise Lost*, for example, are hard to stomach because of the conjunction of two incompatible notions of Deity, of a God of Love who creates free beings who can reject his love and of a God of absolute Power whom none can withstand. Mr. Tolkien is not as great a writer as Milton, but in this matter he has succeeded where Milton failed. As readers of the preceding volumes will remember, the situation in the War of the Ring is as follows: Chance, or Providence, has put the Ring in the hands of the representatives of Good, Elrond, Gandalf, Aragorn. By using it they could destroy Sauron, the incarnation of Evil, but at the cost of becoming his successor. If Sauron recovers the Ring, his victory will be immediate and complete, but even without it his power is greater than any his enemies can bring against him, so that, unless Frodo succeeds in destroying the Ring, Sauron must win.

A PLAUSIBLE REASON FOR EVIL TO LOSE THE WAR

Evil, that is, has every advantage but one—it is inferior in imagination. Good can imagine the possibility of becoming evil—hence the refusal of Gandalf and Aragorn to use the Ring—but Evil, defiantly chosen, can no longer imagine anything but itself. Sauron cannot imagine any motives except lust for dominion and fear so that, when he has learned that his enemies have the Ring, the thought that they might try to destroy it never enters his head, and his eye is kept turned toward Gondor and away from Mordor and the Mount of Doom.

Further, his worship of power is accompanied, as it must be, by anger and a lust for cruelty: learning of Saruman's attempt to steal the Ring for himself, Sauron is so preoccupied with wrath that for two crucial days he pays no attention to a report of spies on the stairs of Cirith Ungol, and when Pippin is foolish enough to look in the palantir of Orthanc, Sauron could have learned all about Frodo's Quest. His wish to capture Pippin and torture the truth from him makes him miss his precious opportunity.

Sauron is not overthrown, however, before many brave men have died and much damage has been done and even his defeat involves loss—the three Elven Rings lose their power and the Elves must leave Middle-earth. Nor is the victory of Good over Evil final: there was Morgoth before Sauron and no one knows what dread successor may afflict the world in ages to come.

The demands made on the writer's powers in an epic as long as *The Lord of the Rings* are enormous and increase as the tale proceeds—the battles have to get more spectacular, the situations more critical, the adventures more thrilling—but I can only say that Mr. Tolkien has proved equal to them. Readers of the previous volumes may be interested to know that Gandalf's hunch about Gollum was right—but for Gollum, the Quest would have failed at the last moment.

From the appendices they will get tantalizing glimpses of the First and Second Ages. The legends of these are, I understand, already written and I hope that, as soon as the publishers have seen *The Lord of the Rings* into a paperback edition, they will not keep Mr. Tolkien's growing army of fans waiting too long.

The Lord of the Rings Is Greatly Overrated

Edmund Wilson

Well-known critic Edmund Wilson chronicled and commented on much of the literature of the twentieth century. He writes that he has read the entire *Lord of the Rings* trilogy to his seven-year-old daughter, a *Hobbit* fan, and does not consider the books to be very well done. Far from being a book for adults, Wilson says, *The Lord of the Rings* is a children's book that got out of hand.

In 1937, Dr. J.R.R. Tolkien, an Oxford don, published a children's book called *The Hobbit*, which had an immense success. The hobbits are a not quite human race who inhabit an imaginary country called the Shire and who combine the characteristics of certain English animals—they live in burrows like rabbits and badgers—with the traits of English country-dwellers, ranging from rustic to tweedy. (The name seems a telescoping of rabbit and Hobbs.) They have elves, trolls and dwarfs as neighbors, and they are associated with a magician called Gandalph and a slimy water-creature called Gollum. Dr. Tolkien became interested in his fairy-tale country and has gone on from this little story to elaborate a long romance, which has appeared, under the general title *The Lord of the Rings*, in three volumes: *The Fellowship of the Ring, The Two Towers* and *The Return of the King*. All volumes are accompanied with maps, and Dr. Tolkien, who is a philologist, professor at Merton College of English Language and Literature, has equipped the last volume with a scholarly apparatus of appendices, explaining the alphabets and grammars of the various tongues spoken by his characters, and giving full genealogies and tables of historical chronology.

Dr. Tolkien has announced that this series—the hypertrophic sequel to *The Hobbit*—is intended for adults rather than chil-

Excerpted from Edmund Wilson, "Oo, Those Awful Orcs," *The Nation*, April 15, 1956. Reprinted with permission.

dren, and it has had a resounding reception at the hands of a number of critics who are certainly grown-up in years. Mr. Richard Hughes, for example, has written of it that nothing of the kind on such a scale has been attempted since *The Faerie Queen*, and that "for width of imagination it almost beggars parallel." ...

A Children's Book That Got Out of Hand

But if one goes from these eulogies to the book itself, one is likely to be let down, astonished, baffled. The reviewer has just read the whole thing aloud to his seven-year-old daughter, who has been through *The Hobbit* countless times, beginning it again the moment she has finished, and whose interest has been held by its more prolix successors. One is puzzled to know why the author should have supposed he was writing for adults. There are, to be sure, some details that are a little unpleasant for a children's book, but except when he is being pedantic and also boring the adult reader, there is little in *The Lord of the Rings* over the head of a seven-year-old child. It is essentially a children's book—a children's book which has somehow got out of hand, since, instead of directing it at the "juvenile" market, the author has indulged himself in developing the fantasy for its own sake; and it ought to be said at this point, before emphasizing its inadequacies as literature, that Dr. Tolkien makes few claims for his fairy romance. In a statement prepared for his publishers, he has explained that he began it to amuse himself, as a philological game: "The invention of languages is the foundation. The 'stories' were made rather to provide a world for the languages than the reverse. I should have preferred to write in 'Elvish.'" He has omitted, he says, in the printed book, a good deal of the philological part; "but there is a great deal of linguistic matter ... included or mythologically expressed in the book. It is to me, anyway, largely an essay in 'linguistic esthetic,' as I sometimes say to people who ask me 'what it is all about.' ... It is not 'about' anything but itself. Certainly it has *no* allegorical intentions, general, particular or topical, moral, religious or political." An overgrown fairy story, a philological curiosity—that is, then, what *The Lord of the Rings* really is. The pretentiousness is all on the part of Dr. Tolkien's infatuated admirers, and it is these pretensions that I would here assail. ...

Both Prose and Verse Are Amateurish

The Lord of the Rings ... is indeed the tale of a Quest, but, to the reviewer, an extremely unrewarding one. The hero has no seri-

ous temptations; is lured by no insidious enchantments, perplexed by few problems. What we get is a simple confrontation
—in more or less the traditional terms of British melodrama—
of the Forces of Evil with the Forces of Good, the remote and
alien villain with the plucky little home-grown hero. There are
streaks of imagination: the ancient tree-spirits, the Ents, with
their deep eyes, twiggy beards, rumbly voices; the Elves, whose
nobility and beauty is elusive and not quite human. But even
these are rather clumsily handled. There is never much development in the episodes; you simply go on getting more of the
same thing. Dr. Tolkien has little skill at narrative and no instinct
for literary form. The characters talk a story-book language that
might have come out of [children's author] Howard Pyle, and as
personalities they do not impose themselves. At the end of this
long romance, I had still no conception of the wizard Gandalph,
who is a cardinal figure, had never been able to visualize him at
all. For the most part such characterizations as Dr. Tolkien is
able to contrive are perfectly stereotyped: Frodo the good little
Englishman, Samwise, his doglike servant, who talks lower-
class and respectful, and never deserts his master. These characters who are no characters are involved in interminable adventures the poverty of invention displayed in which is, it seems
to me, almost pathetic. On the country in which the Hobbits, the
Elves, the Ents and the other Good People live, the Forces of Evil
are closing in, and they have to band together to save it. The hero
is the Hobbit called Frodo who has become possessed of a ring
that Sauron, the King of the Enemy, wants (that learned reptil-
ian suggestion—doesn't it give you a goosefleshy feeling?). In
spite of the author's disclaimer, the struggle for the ring does
seem to have some larger significance. This ring, if one continues to carry it, confers upon one special powers, but it is felt to
become heavier and heavier; it exerts on one a sinister influence
that one has to brace oneself to resist. The problem is for Frodo
to get rid of it before he can succumb to this influence.

Disappointingly Ineffectual "Horrors" Lead to a Flat Climax

Now, this situation does create interest; it does seem to have
possibilities. One looks forward to a queer dilemma, a new
kind of hair-breadth escape, in which Frodo, in the Enemy's
kingdom, will find himself half-seduced into taking over the
enemy's point of view, so that the realm of shadows and horrors will come to seem to him, once he is in it, once he is

strong in the power of the ring, a plausible and pleasant place, and he will narrowly escape the danger of becoming a monster himself. But these bugaboos are not magnetic; they are feeble and rather blank; one does not feel they have any real power. The Good People simply say "Boo" to them. There are Black Riders, of whom everyone is terrified but who never seem anything but specters. There are dreadful hovering birds—think of it, horrible birds of prey! There are ogreish disgusting Orcs, who, however, rarely get to the point of committing any overt acts. There is a giant female spider—a dreadful creepy-crawly spider!—who lives in a dark cave and eats people. What one misses in all these terrors is any trace of concrete reality. The preternatural, to be effective, should be given some sort of solidity, a real presence, recognizable features—like Gulliver, like Gogol, like Poe; not like those phantom horrors of Algernon Blackwood which prove so disappointing after the travel-book substantiality of the landscapes in which he evokes them. Tolkien's horrors resemble these in their lack of real contact with their victims, who dispose of them as we do of the horrors in dreams by simply pushing them or puffing them away. As for Sauron, the ruler of Mordor (doesn't the very name have a shuddery sound?) who concentrates in his person everything that is threatening the Shire, the build-up for him goes on through three volumes. He makes his first, rather promising, appearance as a terrible fire-rimmed yellow eye seen in a water-mirror. But this is as far as we ever get. Once Sauron's realm is invaded, we think we are going to meet him; but he still remains nothing but a burning eye scrutinizing all that occurs from the window of a remote dark tower. This might, of course, be made effective; but actually it is not; we never feel Sauron's power. And the climax, to which we have been working up through exactly nine hundred and ninety-nine large close-printed pages, when it comes, proves extremely flat. The ring is at last got rid of by being dropped into a fiery crater, and the kingdom of Sauron "topples" in a brief and banal earthquake that sets fire to everything and burns it up, and so releases the author from the necessity of telling the reader what exactly was so terrible there. Frodo has come to the end of his Quest, but the reader has remained untouched by the wounds and fatigues of his journey. An impotence of imagination seems to me to sap the whole story. The wars are never dynamic; the or-

NOT "RABBIT" AND "HOBBS"

Tolkien biographer Daniel Grotta reports on the origin of the word "hobbit."

Tolkien was never certain how he came to invent the word "hobbit." It was more spontaneous generation than calculation; certainly, not the combination of "rabbit" and (Thomas) "Hobbes," as the eminent American critic Edmund Wilson speculated. "I don't know where the word came from," admitted Tolkien. "You can't catch your mind out. It might have been associated with Sinclair Lewis' *Babbit*. Certainly not rabbit, as some people think. Babbit has the same bourgeois smugness that hobbits do. His world is the same limited place." Another theory on the origin of the word hobbit is advanced by Paul Kocher, author of *Master of Middle Earth*. According to Kocher, the Oxford English Dictionary defines the Middle English word "hob" (or "hobbe") as a rustic or a clown, a sort of Robin Good-fellow (the English equivalent of the "little people" of Celtic mythology). Since hobbits seem to display many of the characteristics of hobs—small size, simple nature, love of country-side,—then perhaps Tolkien unconsciously transformed a word with which he was undoubtedly familiar into a new creature. In any event, the word "hobbit" is uniquely Tolkien's invention, like "pandemonium" in Milton's *Paradise Lost* and "chortle" in Carroll's *Alice in Wonderland*.

Daniel Grotta, *The Biography of J.R.R. Tolkien: Architect of Middle-Earth*, second edition. Philadelphia: Running Press, 1978.

deals give no sense of strain; the fair ladies would not stir a heartbeat; the horrors would not hurt a fly.

AN APPETITE FOR JUVENILE TRASH

Now, how is it that these long-winded volumes of what looks to this reviewer like balderdash have elicited such tributes as those above? The answer is, I believe, that certain people—especially, perhaps, in Britain—have a lifelong appetite for juvenile trash. They would not accept adult trash, but, confronted with the pre-teen-age article, they revert to the mental phase which delighted in *Elsie Dinsmore* and *Little Lord Fauntleroy* and which seems to have made of Billy Bunter, in England, almost a national figure. You can see it in the tone they fall into when they talk about Tolkien in print: they bubble, they squeal, they coo; they go on about Malory and Spenser—both of whom have a charm and a distinction that Tolkien has never touched.

As for me, if we must read about imaginary kingdoms, give me James Branch Cabell's Poictesme. He at least writes for grown-up people, and he does not present the drama of life as a showdown between Good People and Goblins. He can cover more ground in an episode that lasts only three pages than Tolkien is able to in one of his twenty-page chapters and he can create a more disquieting impression by a reference to something that is never described than Tolkien through his whole demonology.

Tolkien's Understanding and Use of Mythology Create a Profound Effect

Ruth S. Noel

Tolkien made a lifetime study of the world's mythologies, writes Ruth S. Noel. His works were an attempt to revive interest in mythology, and in this he was eminently successful. Noel is the author of *The Mythology of Middle-Earth*, from which this essay is excerpted.

There is something in Professor John Ronald Reuel Tolkien's works that lies deeper than fantasy or escape. This quality is the same as that found in authentic myths and folk tales, a sense generated by the nearly forgotten but potent beliefs and traditions that form the skeleton of old lore. Researchers such as Sir James Frazer have compared and explicated some of these sources, tracing great epics and bedtime stories alike back to the first human struggles to bring order to the world. The sense of depth in Tolkien's works has its source in the author's understanding and selective use of the ancient themes from mythology.

This [essay] discusses some of the purposes of myth, the effect of myth on the development of Middle-earth, and Tolkien's philosophies on myth.

Although primarily a philologist, Tolkien studied mythology for most of his life. He was one of the world's greatest authorities on the Old English and Middle English languages, and was a specialist in Old English and related Teutonic and Celtic lore. With his works he made an eminently successful effort to revive the decreasing interest in mythology. The Teutonic and Celtic mythologies that most interested Tolkien had never been given the emphasis that had been placed upon classical Greek and Roman mythology; Tolkien's works have helped to arouse interest in these areas. This can be seen in the number of recent works based on these myths.

To thoroughly appreciate Tolkien's works, it is necessary to have an understanding of mythology. Unfortunately, the study of mythology itself is a very uncertain one, and it is seldom possible to reconstruct a single clear-cut version of a myth with its sources and purposes neatly set out. Contemporary records of pre-Christian myths are often contradictory or confused. Later accounts of these myths are more coherent, but both the conversion to Christianity and the effort of organizing the material have often biased the telling of ancient lore. So much has been lost from Celtic and Teutonic mythology that it is doubtful that a single, fundamental, and coherent interpretation will ever be made of what remains. Trends in interpretation change, new material is discovered, and, on occasion, old material is found to be unreliable. Only rarely does a comprehensive, scientific inquiry, such as that of Jakob and Wilhelm Grimm into Teutonic mythology, or a dedicated, gifted retelling of the myths, like that of the twelfth-century Icelandic writer Snorri Sturluson, bring mythology alive to the reader.

UNDERSTANDING THE PURPOSES OF MYTHOLOGY

The understanding of mythology requires the understanding of its purposes. The purposes of mythology are to glorify history with supernatural events, to explain the unknown, and to hallow tradition. First, historical myths augment history with supernatural events and divine beings, suggesting that the civilization concerned has been singled out for divine guidance. Second, myths that explain the unknown attempt to bring order to a chaotic conception of the world and to provide formal answers to questions that cannot be answered practically. Third, myths that hallow tradition describe the supernatural circumstances in which the traditions came about, glorifying the traditions in order to perpetuate them. Comparable mythologies have evolved in virtually every culture because man universally faces the same challenges, asks the same questions, and lives in awe of the same forces.

There are two levels of myth in *The Lord of the Rings*. Not only is it written as an epic myth itself, but it also presents the internal mythologies of the peoples of Middle-earth. The three basic purposes of myth are served in these internal mythologies. The histories are peopled with divine and immortal beings, questions about the unknown are given answers, and traditions, are hallowed and maintained.

Tolkien was aware of mythology's purposes and used it meaningfully. His fidelity to the purposes of myth produces a coherent internal mythology for the epic of Middle-earth and provides significant depth for the characterization of both individuals and nations.

THE EFFECTIVENESS OF TOLKIEN'S USE OF MYTH

Tolkien's adaptation of mythology to his works has a profound effect on the reader. This effectiveness is not accidental. Mythic themes deal with basic challenges that face man universally and eternally, such as love, fate, and death. Mythic thought is traceable to the very emergence of human imagination. Such symbolism can be seen in Paleolithic art with its records of ceremonial events and its expressionistic depiction of nature. Even earlier symbolism can be seen in Neanderthal burials, in which the manner of burial was determined by some dawning concept of an afterlife, or imaginative attempt at restoration of life to the dead.

Mythological themes are vastly ancient and are a basic part of the subconscious working of the mind. Thus they have the power to thrill or terrify in the same way that dreams do. In fact, the symbols common in mythology sometimes arise spontaneously in dreams. The study of psychology is doing much to explain the motivation of mythic themes.

Because of the powerful connotation of myth, Tolkien considered mythic themes the most effective way to glorify or debase his characters. An independent author, seldom influenced by his contemporaries, Tolkien must have used his own reactions as a basis for choosing his mythological themes. Sometimes his selections are questionable, such as the apparent death of nearly every important character. Other themes, however, produce a stifling, nightmare horror or a spiritual sense of exultation. The considerable popularity of Tolkien's works attests to the appeal of his selections.

Although the sources of many of Tolkien's themes are to be found in mythology, specific influences are sometimes difficult to trace. Sometimes the theme's source . . . can be located with certainty. Sometimes the theme, such as that of Sauron's powerful, lost Ring, is ubiquitous so that it is difficult to determine a particular source. Sometimes the ideas, such as those concerning the nature of the Elves and Dwarves, are so general that they do not seem to have come from a single source, but rather to have been absorbed through a sort of literary osmosis. In cases of the latter kind, . . . [it] is not intended that all the references should be taken as direct influences on Tolkien's writing. On the other hand, it is more than likely that Tolkien was familiar with all of them.

TOLKIEN'S WORKS FORM THEIR OWN GENRE

Tolkien's works form a continuation of the mythic tradition into modern literature. For this reason they form a genre by themselves. In no other literary work has such a careful balance of mythic tradition and individual imagination been maintained. Authors who have been compared with Tolkien emphasize either the mythic or the imaginative side of their works to the detriment of the other. Tolkien, however, maintains a consistent homogeneity.

Throughout the works, the fiction is maintained that the prehistoric chronology of the Third Age of Middle-earth is the source of the mythologies we know. Tolkien excuses his use of names and themes from historic mythology on the basis that *The Lord of the Rings* tells the true story, imperfectly remembered in our historic lore. Bilbo's song, "There is an inn," sung by Frodo, is a good example: Tolkien presents what he pretends is the original form of the nursery rhyme "Hey diddle diddle," where the cow jumps over the moon.

The adaptation of mythological themes to imaginative fiction is a difficult challenge. Mythology is a conservative medium: myths are always repeated in a traditional way, rather than being casually left to the teller's whim. However, the constant retelling of myths over hundreds, even thousands, of years wears them smooth, concentrates them, until everything superfluous is worn away. In contrast, modern literature is dependent on innovation and creativity for its success. In combining the two literary philosophies, Tolkien produced a myth that is coherent and readable from the modern point of view, and a work of imaginative fiction made concrete by its basis in the ancient and universal language of myth. The result of the combination is sometimes

self-conscious, forced, and unwieldy, but much of it is remarkably vivid, dimensional, and evocative.

THE QUALITIES OF MIDDLE-EARTH

The success of Tolkien's works is based on the vividness, di-
mensionality, and evocative qualities of Middle-earth. To say
Middle-earth was created by Tolkien would be an oversim-
plification. Instead, Middle-earth exists on three levels. First,
it is the actual continent of Europe, with landscapes, vegetation, animal life, and some of man's ancient works, taken
from reality. Second, Middle-earth is the product of the poetic imagination of the early Europeans, who peopled the
mountains, forest, and sea with divine, semidivine, and de-
monic beings. Finally, Tolkien superimposed his imagination on the lands and their natural and supernatural inhabitants, enhancing the mood of the landscape and deepening
the character of its peoples.

Whatever Middle-earth is, it is not Faerie. It is not, as
Faerie is said to be, a remote, inviolable land of indescribable beauty. There are isolated fragments of Faerie, or rather
reconstructions of it, in Tolkien's Middle-earth, in such
places as Lórien. On the whole, however, there is very little
of the supernatural in the geography of Middle-earth.

Nevertheless, there is a curiously timeless quality about
Middle-earth. Its history spans thousands of years, and the
time of the War of the Ring is apparently both prehistoric
and pagan, although the primary culture is feudal and such
anachronisms as coffee and potatoes have intruded. This
sense of mingled time-frames is reminiscent of that of Malory's *Le Morte Darthur*, a resemblance that may not be accidental. In *Le Morte Darthur*, myths about Celtic gods are attributed to the approximately fifth-century King Arthur, but
are set in the culture and language of medieval chivalry. The
result in both Malory's and Tolkien's works is a curiously
opposite suspension of time. *The Lord of the Rings* appears
to have the timelessness the hobbits ascribed to Lórien: "as
if inside a song a medieval song sung to a pagan tune.

TOLKIEN'S ESSAY "ON FAIRY-STORIES"

The best available guide to what Tolkien felt about the
mythology that inspired his works is found in his essay "On
Fairy-Stories." Tolkien wrote this essay at the time he was
beginning *The Lord of the Rings*, and it later appeared in the

book *Tree and Leaf.* In view of the way *The Lord of the Rings* finally developed, the essay's insights on magic, *eucatastrophe*, and justice are particularly valuable.

The magic Tolkien admired was magic devoid of sleight-of-hand fakery, mystery uncontaminated by cloak-and-dagger sensationalism, and miracle unconfined to orthodox religion. The purpose of this magic is to exercise the sense of wonder and to fulfill wish. Magic is the process which produces eucatastrophe.

Eucatastrophe is Tolkien's word for the anti-catastrophic "turn" (*strophe* in Greek) that characterizes fairy stories. This turning occurs when imminent evil is unexpectedly averted and great good succeeds. To Tolkien, tragedy was the purest form of drama, while eucatastrophe, the antithesis of tragedy, was the purest form of the fairy story. In "On Fairy-Stories," Tolkien gives the purpose and effect of eucatastrophe: "It does not deny the existence . . . of sorrow and failure . . . it denies universal final defeat . . . giving a fleeting glimpse of Joy, Joy beyond the walls of the world, poignant as grief."

To Tolkien, the most satisfying form of eucatastrophe, and that which he developed to the greatest extent in his works, was denial of death. This concept is basic to Christianity, but also plays an important part in pagan myth. The desire for eternal life runs deep in the human imagination—burial practices of even some Neanderthal peoples reflect a hope of life beyond the grave. Sometimes, as in Scandinavian mythology, the afterlife was visualized as a continuation of earthly life: in Odin's hall, warriors fought and feasted until the end of the world. The fighting and feasting were an important part of the Celtic afterlife as well, but the Celts added a significant element in their lyrical descriptions of the unearthly beauty and joy of the otherworld. However, it is not the physical aspect of the afterworld, or the events that take place there, that are important. (Tolkien wisely gave only the most sparse account of the Blessed Realm.) The need is to believe, even briefly or metaphorically, that death can be denied, even with the recognition of the necessary departure from the living world. This is the eucatastrophe from old lore which Tolkien has striven to supply.

Another theme that Tolkien found in fairy stories was justice. In his own works, it is unfailingly meted out, although he sparingly doles out the deepest doom, death, never giving it to any character introduced by name except as punishment for inexpiable sins or as a victorious resolution of all life's conflicts.

Tolkien's adherence to justice and mercy is his greatest concession to the Christian philosophy. For a dedicatedly Christian author, Tolkien wrote an unusually sympathetic account of a pagan world. The combination is again reminiscent of Malory's *Le Morte Darthur*, where pagan themes, motives, and moods are interspersed with Christian ideals.

REALISM VS. JUSTICE AND MERCY

Despite Tolkien's statement to the contrary, justice is not inherent in fairy stories. For example, he said that "The Frog Prince" is about the importance of keeping promises. In the version collected by Jakob and Wilhelm Grimm, the princess indeed promised the frog a place by her dish and on her pillow if he recovered her golden ball. But when he came for his reward, she angrily dashed him against the wall. He became a prince thereupon, and married the disloyal and undeserving princess. This sort of caprice of fate is as common in folk tales as is justice.

The emphasis on fate rather than on justice is as much the hallmark of modernism in literature as it was of pre-Christian myth. It is no longer necessary for a work of fiction to come to a conclusion that satisfies the desire for justice or mercy. It is not even necessary to reach any resolution. The same effect occurs in myth when the favor of the gods is bestowed or withdrawn arbitrarily. This point of view is one of realism: justice and mercy are less facts than spiritual ideals.

Tolkien demonstrated this in his overall view of the quest, where he showed justice to be a goal—unrealized but attainable. He gave two roles to justice in view of his combination of pagan fatalism and Judeo-Christian ethics. In the pagan sense, justice is to be striven for so that one may meet fate honorably. In the Judeo-Christian sense, it is sought in order that one may reject evil. Appropriately to these two roles, Tolkien resolved the story in two directions, with the idealist, Frodo, departing to eternal life beyond the world, and the realist, Samwise, returning to the center of the world's life, the hearth of home.

Tolkien Fails to Achieve His Artistic Goals in *The Lord of the Rings*

C.N. Manlove

In his essay "On Fairy-Stories," Tolkien spelled out his conception of "Recovery," the necessity for a writer to produce a new perception in his work. C.N. Manlove examines Tolkien's concept of "Recovery" and concludes that while the author is moderately successful in parts of *The Lord of the Rings* his flat descriptions and poor characterizations reveal a general failure to achieve his artistic aims. Manlove is a lecturer in English literature at the University of Edinburgh, Scotland.

Tolkien's stylistic aims are associated with his conception of 'Recovery': the writer is to generalize and depersonalize his descriptions (though not emasculate them) to make them universally available. The reader will hopefully come thereby to a fresh view of objects he has long taken for granted, and through that to a recovery of what are for him their archetypes. Sensibility is thus not to be extended so much as reminded:

> However good in themselves, illustrations do little good to fairy-stories. The radical distinction between all art (including drama) that offers a *visible* presentation and true literature is that it imposes one visible form. Literature works from mind to mind and thus is more progenitive. It is at once more universal and more poignantly particular. If it speaks of *bread* or *wine* or *stone* or *tree*, it appeals to the whole of these things, to their ideas; yet each hearer will give to them a peculiar personal embodiment in his imagination. Should the story say 'he ate bread', the dramatic producer or painter can only show 'a piece of bread' according to his taste or fancy, but the hearer of the story will think of bread in general and picture it in some form of his own. If a story says, "he climbed a hill

Excerpted from *Modern Fantasy: Five Studies*, by C.N. Manlove (New York: Cambridge University Press, 1975). Reprinted by permission of the author.

and saw a river in the valley below', the illustrator may catch, or nearly catch, his own vision of such a scene; but every hearer of the words will have his own picture, and it will be made out of all the hills and rivers and dales he has ever seen, but specially out of The Hill, The River, The Valley which were for him the first embodiment of the word. (*TL*, p. 67)[1]

The method can be seen best in the description of Lothlórien (without doubt the finest set-piece in the book).[2] When Frodo arrives at Cerin Amroth, he sees

> a great mound, covered with a sward of grass as green as Spring-time in the Elder days. Upon it, as a double crown, grew two circles of trees: the outer had bark of snowy white, and were leafless but beautiful in their shapely nakedness; the inner were mallorn-trees of great height, still arrayed in pale gold. High amid the branches of a towering tree that stood in the centre of all there gleamed a white flet. At the feet of the trees, and all about the green hillsides the grass was studded with small golden flowers shaped like stars. Among them, nodding on slender stalks, were other flowers, white and palest green: they glimmered as a mist amid the rich hue of the grass. Over all the sky was blue, and the sun of afternoon glowed upon the hill and cast long green shadows beneath the trees. (*LR*, I, 364–5)[3]

... Our subconscious has been here before, and Tolkien has only to beckon it in. Hence the vagueness of the account. First the mound seems to be wholly covered with the grass, and then we are told it was crowned with trees: this begins the blurring. Then the grass was 'as green as Spring-time in the Elder days'. Its green colour becomes conceptualized: spring is only metaphorically green. As for the Elder days, we know nothing of spring then, but we are being asked to imagine. The trees seem more specific, but the two circles evoke the archetype of the secret centre, and the white circle about the gold seems as 'right' as the yolk of an egg surrounded by the white.[4] Then, with the towering tree, we reach, as we desire, the hub; to return outwards to the flowers which we see as a mass. We do not see the white trees: they are 'beautiful in their shapely nakedness', but what that means, our subconscious must tell us. The flowers are described as 'golden flowers shaped like stars', 'white and palest green', but they are so much anyone's 'idea' of a flower that they do not stand out; so too with the blue sky, the sun, and the long green shadows. It is finely done. Tolkien indicates the desired response in Frobo's 'He saw no colour but those he knew, gold and white and blue and green, but they were fresh and poignant, as if he had at that moment first perceived them and made for them names new and wonderful' (*LR*, I, 365).

The stylistic aim of 'Recovery' may also explain why the landscapes of *The Lord of the Rings* are both elemental and repetitive. There are three main mountain ranges, the Misty Mountains, the Emyn Muil and the Mountains of Mordor, all of them barriers to progress, all similar in height and all young, jagged and rocky. There are three main towers (the White Tower of Minas Tirith, Orthanc and Barad-dûr); two rather similarly constructed cities (though one is of living wood and the other of stone)—the City of the Galadrim and Minas Tirith; three tunnels through mountains, each fraught with horror (that through Moria, the Paths of the Dead and the Pass of Cirith Ungol); three plains (the Brown Lands, the grasslands of Rohan and the plain of Gorgoroth); and three forests (the Old Forest, Lothlórien and Fangorn). Through our experience of these, Tolkien would presumably hope that our archetypal images of The Hill, The Mountain, The Forest, The Plain and The Tower will be more surely brought to life in our minds.

The usually absolute distinctions between good and evil[5] may also be a function of this technique: to come at the 'this-ness' of a thing, it must be presented pure. Thus for example every detail about the orcs—their squat appearance (*LR*, II, 50, 138), crooked legs (II, 50), hairy arms (II, 58), swart or sallow faces (I, 339; II, 171), bad breath (II, 58), loathsome foods (II, 54; III, 190), hideous dialects (II, 48), even their harsh medicine (II, 51, 52)—points in one direction, and is aimed at producing one response: loathing. The same method to reverse effect is seen with the good. This polari-zation may well be intended to make it easier for the reader to grasp essences. Those like Edmund Wilson who complain that Tolkien has nothing new to say about good and evil[6] would then have missed the point.

It is possible, again, that the style required for 'Recovery' explains the use of simile (which leaves the terms discrete) rather than metaphor in *The Lord of the Rings*. The 'stock' nature, too, of such similes may be part of this style. Bilbo leaves his home at Bag End 'like a rustle of wind in the grass' (*LR*, I, 44); the piled spears of the Rohirrim, the warriors of Rohan, bristle 'like thickets of new-planted trees' (III, 67; see also II, 129); the Ents, in Isengard, 'went striding and storming like a howling gale, breaking pillars ... tossing up huge slabs of stone into the air like leaves' (II, 173); when Aragorn dismisses the Host of the Dead, they 'vanished like a mist that is driven back by a sudden wind' (III, 153); as Frodo and Sam approach Mount Doom, Barad-dûr grows nearer 'like the oncoming of a wall of night at the last end of the world' (III, 212).

Some similes are, however, constantly repeated, so frequently that not even a ritualistic function seems adequate to account for them. The Elves are invariably associated with starlight (*LR*, I, 221, 369, 380; II, 339), particularly their eyes (I, 239; III, 310); mountain ranges and standing-stones always look like teeth (I, 141, 416; III, 68); the orcs and Gollum appear as insects, especially spiders (I, 416; II, 147, 220, 244, 253; III, 227); whenever a battle-onslaught is described, the analogy of a wave is used (II, 138, 140, 142; III, 112, 119, 226). One feels here in fact that Tolkien could have found some different terms for his figures instead of wearing the same trope to a shadow.

All the features of the book that we have examined may fit in with Tolkien's stylistic intentions,[7] but the question of whether they come over powerfully is another matter. To write a generalized style is not to escape having to write well: Lothlórien succeeds as a picture not because it is non-specific, but because it is done with skill. An 'archetypal' aesthetic is no excuse for an anaemic performance. It is in this light that we must now consider Tolkien's method.

REPETITIVE AND AMBIGUOUS DESCRIPTIONS OF CHARACTERS

This is the picture he offers us of Celeborn and Galadriel, the Lord and Lady of Lothlórien,

> Very tall they were, and the Lady no less tall than the Lord; and they were grave and beautiful. They were clad wholly in white; and the hair of the Lady was of deep gold, and the hair of the Lord Celeborn was of silver long and bright; but no sign of age was upon them, unless it were in the depths of their eyes; for these were keen as lances in the starlight, and yet profound, the wells of deep memory. (*LR*, I, 369)

We are not told how tall they were, nor is there any detail about their clothing apart from its whiteness which would help us to see it. The contrasting colours of their hair only brings us to the verge of seeing the Rich, Full Woman and the Grave, Elderly Man—a verge from which we are thrust

"RECOVERY"

Tolkien expresses his desire to see things as they should be seen in this excerpt from his essay "On Fairy-Stories."

We should look at green again, and be startled anew (but not blinded) by blue and yellow and red. We should meet the centaur and the dragon, and then perhaps suddenly behold, like the ancient shepherds, sheep, and dogs, and horses—and wolves. This recovery fairy-stories help us to make. In that sense only a taste for them may make us, or keep us, childish.

Recovery (which includes return and renewal of health) is a re-gaining—regaining of a clear view. I do not say "seeing things as they are" and involve myself with the philosophers, though I might venture to say "seeing things as we are (or were) meant to see them"—as things apart from ourselves. We need, in any case, to clean our windows; so that the things seen clearly may be freed from the drab blur of triteness or familiarity—from possessiveness.

J.R.R. Tolkien, "On Fairy-Stories," *Tree and Leaf*. London: Allen & Unwin, 1964.

back, because though Tolkien seems at first to have mentioned the silver hair as a sign of age, he in fact goes on to deny this, 'no sign of age was upon them'. The method here seems almost one of shifting us away from any certainty in the portrayal. Tolkien tells us that they did not look old, unless one looked at the depths of their eyes, but then deals with the surface of the eyes first, going on, '*for* these were keen as lances', before returning us to his original point. Yet at the same time he is asking us to accept a quite complex situation: that their eyes were both extroverted and introverted. His generalized style is of little use in making us feel complex effects like this. Nor, morever, is it good enough even by the standards of the 'Stock Response'. Granted an 'archetypal' method, the archetypes still have to be vividly realized and felt. Yet the portrait of Galadriel and Celeborn lacks wholeness and power, is without the certainty and vigour with which any art worth its salt must be informed.

Hair, eyes and dress—these are the features Tolkien fixes on continually in his portrayals; and in most of them he repeats the idea of eyes being both sharp and profound. Thus Arwen, daughter of Elrond the Elf-King,

Young she was and yet not so. The braids of her dark hair were touched by no frost, her white arms and clear face were flawless and smooth, and the light of stars was in her bright

eyes, grey as a cloudless night; yet queenly she looked, and
thought and knowledge were in her glance, as of one who has
known many things that the years bring. Above her brow her
head was covered with a cap of silver lace netted with small
gems, glittering white; but her soft grey raiment had no or-
nament save a girdle of leaves wrought in silver. (*LR*, I, 239)

And of Éowyn, Théoden's niece,

Grave and thoughtful was her glance.... Very fair was her
face, and her long hair was like a river of gold. Slender and
tall she was in her white robe girt with silver; but strong she
seemed and stern as steel, a daughter of kings ... fair and
cold, like a morning of pale spring that is not yet come to
womanhood. (*LR*, II, 119)

The picture of Arwen has little to offer that that of Galadriel
does not give us. We start with the concept of the 'old-young
woman': though this is better done than before, in that the
contrast is not left to the eyes to make themselves, but is between them and her whole physical appearance, it is still a
repetition. Moreover, words are not really working: to say
her white arms and clear face were flawless and smooth is
to say something twice. And are cloudless nights grey? As for
the analogies between human figures and nature—'frost',
'light of stars', 'cloudless night', 'hair like a river', 'fair and
cold, like a morning of pale spring'—these are no doubt
functions of a general pattern of imagery in the trilogy, but
here the piling of them seems only the result of an inability
to concentrate on the human figure alone and to see it
vividly; indeed Tolkien seems to have lost track of what he
is supposed to be describing when he talks of 'pale spring
that is not yet come to womanhood'. Further, the hair
'touched by frost' comes over not so much 'nature imagery'
as awkwardly precious.

   With many of the characters the descriptions we have are
often perfunctory: so much so that in fact there is very little
to differentiate them. Boromir, we are told, is 'a tall man
with a fair and noble face, dark-haired and grey-eyed, proud
and stern of glance' (*LR*, I, 253); Aragorn, slightly taller and
of slimmer build (I, 305), is otherwise a man with 'a shaggy
head of dark hair flecked with grey, and in a pale stern face
a pair of keen grey eyes' (I, 169); and the men of Gondor,
Mablung and Damrod, are 'goodly men, pale-skinned, dark of
hair, with grey eyes and faces sad and proud' (II, 267). With
the dwarf Gimli and the Elf Legolas we have not even this:
Legolas is introduced to us as 'a strange Elf clad in green

and brown' (I, 253); and Gimli is 'a younger dwarf at Glóin's side—his son Gimli' (ib.). Possibly, though, Tolkien intends the names to be suggestive here: Legolas perhaps conveys the slender and vigorous, and Gimli the short and determined (bradawl overtones!); or else he hopes that the words 'Elf' or 'dwarf' will do their work unaided. Yet he could have done much more. One is not asking for a particular Elf, or even one that can be seen: only for a sense of Elfishness, or any sense at all that the creation has been left.

It may be that Tolkien was aiming at a kind of moral characterization which precludes any physical description, but he does not seem to have felt the morality very powerfully either. Glorfindel the Elf-lord is thus described, 'Glorfindel was tall and straight; his hair was of shining gold, his face fair and young and fearless and full of joy; his eyes were bright and keen, and his voice like music; on his brow sat wisdom, and in his hand was strength' (*LR*, I, 239). The account becomes directly conceptual: all the items are functions of a moral portrayal; to say his hair was of shining gold is not so much to say anything about his hair as to comment on what he stands for. But each item appears in a dead list: one feels not that Tolkien is inside the character working out, but outside it, trying, though not very strenuously, to get in.

SELF-CONSCIOUS WRITING DISTANCES THE READER

Unfortunately, and in a strange way, even when Tolkien really does try to get in, the result is embarrassing. He has a romantic longing to be a part of what he sees as the heroism and beauty of the world of his fantasy, but in fact these are no real part of his experience. The result can be seen in this typical instance taken from the charge of the horsemen of Rohan in defence of beleaguered Minas Tirith,

> Suddenly the king cried to Snowmane and the horse sprang away. Behind him his banner blew in the wind, white horse upon a field of green, but he outpaced it. After him thundered the knights of his house, but he was ever before them. Éomer rode there, the white horsetail on his helm floating in his speed, and the front of the first *éored* roared like a breaker foaming to the shore, but Théoden could not be overtaken. Fey he seemed, or the battle-fury of his fathers ran like new fire in his veins, and he was borne up on Snowmane like a god of old, even as Oromë the Great in the battle of the Valar when the world was young. His golden shield was uncovered, and lo! it shone like an image of the Sun, and the grass flamed into green about the white feet of his steed. For morn-

ing came, morning and a wind from the sea; and darkness
was removed, and the hosts of Mordor wailed, and terror took
them, and they fled, and died, and the hoofs of wrath rode
over them. And then all the host of Rohan burst into song, and
they sang as they slew, for the joy of battle was on them, and
the sound of their singing that was fair and terrible came
even to the City. (*LR*, III, 112–13)

Every word and cadence carries a gush of *voulu* emotion
and hits a false note; this 'joy of battle' is the joy of someone
who has never been in this kind of battle. A few pages later
we find an image, dear to romantic hearts, of Taillefer (the
Norman supposed to have walked at the head of William's
army at Hastings, singing and throwing a jewelled axe in the
air), when Éomer sees the rescuing fleet, 'And then wonder
took him, and a great joy; and he cast his sword up in the
sunlight and sang as he caught it' (*LR*, III, 123). It is self-
conscious: there is a self to be conscious that it is not a part
of it. And it is, incidentally, an obstruction to the reader's response. Tolkien so gets in the way with these excited cries
that he becomes the sole audience of what he describes;[8]
once more, and in a different way, the reader loses touch
with the characters and the material of the fantasy.

ACTION IS RARELY USED TO DEFINE OR DIFFERENTIATE CHARACTERS

Nor do we get much sense of character through the action of
the book. The best we are given for the Fellowship as a
whole is the description of the different sounds of their foot-
steps as they journey in the darkness of Moria, 'the dull
stump of Gimli's dwarf-boots; the heavy tread of Boromir;
the light step of Legolas; the soft, scarce-heard patter of
hobbit-feet; and in the rear the slow firm footfalls of Aragorn
with his long stride' (*LR*, I, 325). And behind that Frodo
thinks he hears 'the faint fall of soft bare feet'. But elsewhere
there is nothing that any of them do which is the peculiar result of being a hobbit or a dwarf or a Gondor man. Frodo
succeeds by virtue both of the smallness and the stubborn
courage which hobbits have, but this is not what one means
by racial peculiarity nor, given Gimli's nature, are hobbits
the only people to show these features. As if aware of this,
Tolkien sometimes tries to impose characteristics on to the
people of his fantasy. When the hobbits Pippin and Merry
are found by Gandalf and the others sitting in the ruins of
Isengard smoking their pipes, and Théoden says he did not

know hobbits smoked, Merry launches forth on a history of how the custom grew up in the Shire; upon which,

> 'You do not know your danger, Théoden,' interrupted Gandalf. 'These hobbits will sit on the edge of ruin and discuss the pleasures of the table, or the small doings of their fathers, grandfathers, and great-grandfathers, and remoter cousins to the ninth degree, if you encourage them with undue patience. Some other time.' (*LR*, II, 163–4; see also III, 146–7)

But the attempt to make the hobbits into quaint and endearing characters is too isolated to succeed; we would not need this account if we had been given any real sense of hobbit peculiarities before. One feels a bit awkward: it is not surprising Tolkien rushes on. The badinage between Gimli, Legolas and the hobbits on the same occasion is similarly sudden and nervous. Gimli's love of mines and stone is more consistently presented: his lament over Durin in the mines of the dwarves at Khazad-dûm and his pleasure in the hard rock of the Hornburg are fine (*LR*, I, 329–30; II, 137). But these special features are pinned on without ever being expressed in action, and invariably occur in fleeting interludes. Since they have no links with the surrounding material to direct them, they often become overpitched, as in Gimli's paean to Legolas on the caverns of Helm's Deep (II, 152–3), or his too-violent worship of Galadriel (II, 35, 118; III, 253). The appendices to *The Lord of the Rings* on the lore, genealogies and languages of the various races of Middle-earth are partly an attempt at the imposition of character by scholarship.[9]

A Weak Vision Does Not "Recover" Freshness

The weakness of the characterization in Tolkien's fantasy frustrates one of his primary aims. For he set out to recover for us in his book a freshness of vision which we are without; and if there is no vision, there can be no freshness. The way the characters tend to run together into a nondescript soup is also precisely counter to the moral polarity he has set up within his fantasy. His picture of the alliance of the peoples of Middle-earth against Sauron is one of a co-operative effort by different races, each with a separate identity, in which the author at least goes through the motions of taking a delight. It is precisely that they retain their generic individualities in coming together that should define the good; and under Sauron and the power of the Ring that identity should fade (*LR*, I, 56). . . .

THE FORCES OF DARKNESS MEAN MORE TO TOLKIEN

As far as Tolkien's descriptions of the 'good' characters in his book are concerned: one gets the impression that he has not really experienced what he is describing, or else that it does not really matter to him. With the evil figures and land-scapes of his fantasy it is different. In the portrait of Shelob, for example, there is a marked increase of pressure,

> [Sam] saw suddenly, issuing from a black hole of shadow un-der the cliff, the most loathly shape that he had ever beheld, horrible beyond the horror of an evil dream. Most like a spi-der she was, but huger than the great hunting beasts, and more terrible than they because of the evil purpose in her re-morseless eyes. Those same eyes that he had thought daunted and defeated, there they were lit with a fell light again, clus-tering in her out-thrust head. Great horns she had, and be-hind her short stalk-like neck was her huge swollen body, a vast bloated bag, swaying and sagging between her legs; its great bulk was black, blotched with livid marks, but the belly underneath was pale and luminous and gave forth a stench. Her legs were bent, with great knobbed joints high above her back, and hairs that stuck out like steel spines, and at each leg's end there was a claw.
>
> As soon as she had squeezed her soft squelching body and its folded limbs out of the upper exit from her lair, she moved with a horrible speed, now running on her creaking legs, now making a sudden bound. (II, 334)[10]

Here all the details are fused in one intense reaction, horror and loathing. It is not, by the way, that we the readers re-spond more easily to evil than to good, but the fact that Tolkien has done so first that is the case here. This is not so with *all* the evil characters: the orcs are not very well real-ized; but on the whole it can be said that the forces of dark-ness mean more to Tolkien than those of light. For all the de-struction of the Dark Lord and his powers, the vision of *The Lord of the Rings* remains peculiarly Manichaean. . . .

There are further drawbacks to *The Lord of the Rings*, not the least of which, given the flabbiness of material, and al-lowing for the sense of scale demanded by epic, is its length. The epithet 'endless worm' coined by one critic seems only too apt.[11] Doubtless there is such a thing as the sheer num-ber of pages the reader has had to turn that can add poignancy to the story—one almost feels this is the case as we come to the great close of Malory's epic. But not with Tolkien's book, for we have never been very much involved anyway. Perhaps also the length of the story and the time he took to write it go some way towards explaining his failure of detachment: his involvement in Middle-earth may well have increased in direct proportion to the time and space at his disposal. Certainly he manages to avoid this fault in his short stories. . . .

It would be easy to conclude that all this results from Tolkien's having been sentimental, evasive and morally uncertain as a man and inadequate as an artist. Yet the weakness of *The Lord of the Rings* may equally come from the fact that he did not express himself fully. The book was largely born out of a reaction against the modern world in which he lived: nostalgia and wish-fulfilment, which were only one part of Tolkien the man, are its essence. That there was more to the author than the work shows can be argued from its very poverty of realization: Tolkien may have found that the good, the beautiful and the age-old did not excite him so much or so plainly as he liked to believe. It is possible that his work becomes facile and weak because of an oversimple judgement on the modern world which is its source and end. *The Lord of the Rings* would thus be a picture rather of Tolkien's uncertainty than of Tolkien himself.

NOTES

1. *TL.* J.R.R. Tolkien, *Tree and Leaf* (Allen & Unwin, 1964).
2. Possibly it owes much to Milton's description of Paradise, or alternatively even to C.S. Lewis' account of Milton's technique in his *A Preface to 'Paradise Lost'* (1942), pp. 46–50.
3. *LR.* J.R.R. Tolkien, *The Lord of the Rings*, 3 vols., 2nd ed. (Allen & Unwin, 1966).
4. On the mandala archetype suggested here, see C.G. Jung, 'Concerning Mandala Symbolism', and 'Mandalas', *The Archetypes and the Collective Unconscious*, in *The Collected Works of C.G. Jung*, trans. R.F.C. Hull, 2nd ed. (Routledge & Kegan Paul, 1969), IX, i, 355–90.
5. There are exceptions among the secondary characters—Boromir, Théoden (at first), Denethor, Saruman and Gollum—and it will be noticed that all of these are killed off.
6. 'Oo, Those Awful Orcs!'; repr. in Edmund Wilson, *The Bit Between My Teeth* (W.H. Allen, N.Y., 1966), pp. 326–32.
7. In a sense even the derivative character of the book, its roots in earlier literature, could be seen as part of 'Recovery': the familiar is being made new.

8. In his 'The Homecoming of Beorhtnoth Beorhthelm's Son', *Essays and Studies*, n.s. VI (1953), 1–18, Tolkien partly condemns this ignorant romantic enthusiasm: we are shown how the young man Torhthelm, who glories in heroism however rash, and indulges in heady sentiments, has lost touch with the real world of suffering and struggle that the older Tídwald knows. Heroism has a place, Tolkien says, only when it has a firm grip on the real world. The imbalance in *The Lord of the Rings* invites parody—and has received it in the *Harvard Lampoon* (by Henry N. Beard and Douglas C. Kenney) *Bored of the Rings* (Signet Books, N.Y., 1969).

9. Cf. Spacks, in N.D. Isaacs and R.A. Zimbardo, eds., *Tolkien and the Critics, Essays on J.R.R. Tolkien's* The Lord of the Rings (Notre Dame, Indiana, 1969), p. 98, 'rhetoric and . . . references seem automatic. . . . All too often, Tolkien asserts rather than demonstrates character'; and Roger Sale, 'Tolkien and Frodo Baggins', *Tolkien and the Critics*, pp. 266–8, 269–70.

10. On spiders, see Tolkien in Charlotte and Denis Plimmer, 'The Man who understands Hobbits', *Daily Telegraph Magazine* (22 March 1968), p. 31: '"Spiders . . . are the particular terror of northern imaginations"'; '"The female monster is certainly no deadlier than the male, but she is different. She is a sucking, strangling, trapping creature.'" See also J.R.R. Tolkien, *The Hobbit*, 2nd ed. (Allen & Unwin, 1951), ch. viii. One critic has seen the portrayal of Shelob, who is, she says, impaled by Sam's knife 'somewhere in the region of the womb', as a picture of Tolkien's 'subtle contempt and hostility towards women' (Catherine R. Stimpson, *J.R.R. Tolkien*, Columbia Essays on Modern Writers, no. 41 (Columbia Univ. Press, N.Y., 1969, 19).

11. Maurice Richardson, 'New Novels', *New Statesman and Nation* (18 Dec. 1954), p. 836, 'My first impression is that it [*The Two Towers*] is all far too long and blown up. What began as a charming children's book has proliferated into an endless worm.' See also Mark Roberts, 'Adventure in English', *Essays in Criticism*, VI (1956), p. 459. Tolkien, however, thought that the great defect of his epic was that it was too short (*LR*, I, 6).

Tolkien's Sources: The True Tradition

T.A. Shippey

Although Tolkien disapproved of academics' tracing the literary influences on particular works, T.A. Shippey argues that a familiarity with the literature Tolkien drew on in writing The Lord of the Rings *can only enhance the reader's understanding and enjoyment. Shippey identifies sources from ancient writings such as* Beowulf *through modern authors. This essay is an appendix in Shippey's book* The Road to Middle-Earth.

Tolkien himself did not approve of the academic search for 'sources'. He thought it tended to distract attention from the work of art itself, and to undervalue the artist by the suggestion that he had 'got it all' from somewhere else. This [essay] accordingly does not attempt to match 'source' to 'passage' in Tolkien. It does however offer a brief guide to the works which nourished Tolkien's imagination and to which he returned again and again; since many of them are not well known, this may give many people who have enjoyed Tolkien something else to enjoy. Whether that changes their reading of *The Lord of the Rings* or *The Silmarillion* is less important: though in fact comparison with 'the sources', in my experience, almost always brings out Tolkien's extremely keen eye for the vital detail.

He was also very quick to detect the bogus and the anachronistic, which is why I use the phrase '*true* tradition'. Tolkien was irritated all his life by modern attempts to rewrite or interpret old material, almost all of which he thought led to failures of tone and spirit. Wagner is the most obvious example. People were always connecting *The Lord of the Rings* with *Der Ring des Nibelungen*, and Tolkien did not like it. 'Both rings were round', he snarled, 'and there the resemblance ceases' (*Letters*, p. 306). This is not entirely true. The motifs of the riddle-contest, the

Excerpted from *The Road to Middle-Earth*, by T.A. Shippey (London: George Allen & Unwin). Copyright © 1982 by T.A. Shippey. Reprinted by permission of A.P. Watt on behalf of T.A. Shippey.

cleansing fire, the broken weapon preserved for an heir, all occur in both works, as of course does the theme of 'the lord of the
Ring as the slave of the Ring', *des Ringes Herr als des Ringes
Knecht.* But what upset Tolkien was the fact that Wagner was
working, at second-hand, from material which *he* knew at first-
hand, primarily the heroic poems of the *Elder Edda* and the
later Middle High German *Nibelungenlied.* Once again he saw
difference where other people saw similarity. Wagner was one
of several authors with whom Tolkien had a relationship of in-
timate dislike: Shakespeare, Spenser, George MacDonald, Hans
Christian Andersen. All, he thought, had got something very important not quite right. It is especially necessary, then, for followers of Tolkien to pick out the true from the heretical, and to
avoid snatching at surface similarities.

OLD ENGLISH SOURCES

The single work which influenced Tolkien most was obviously the Old English poem *Beowulf*, written in Tolkien's
opinion somewhere round the year 700. The best edition of
this is by F. Klaeber (1950). There are many translations of
it, including the one by J.R. Clark Hall and C.L. Wrenn to
which Tolkien wrote the 'Preface' in 1940. The reasons for
its appeal to him, however, seem to me to be expressed best
in R.W. Chambers, *Beowulf: an Introduction* (1959). The first
two chapters of this show with particular force and charm
the way in which history and fairy-tale are in *Beowulf* inter-
twined. Other Old English poems which Tolkien used include *The Ruin, The Wanderer* and *The Battle of Maldon*, all
conveniently edited and translated in Richard Hamer's *A
Choice of Anglo-Saxon Verse* (1970), and the 'Treebeard-
style' gnomic poems *Maxims I* and *II*, edited and translated,
along with *Solomon and Saturn II*, in my *Poems of Wisdom
and Learning in Old English* (1976). Tolkien's own edition
and translation of the poem *Exodus*, prepared for publication by Joan Turville-Petre, [was] published by Oxford University Press in 1981. Significantly enough, Tolkien valued
the work as an example of Christian material treated in an
old-fashioned or heroic style; his own fiction, one might ar-
gue, was a similar mixture but the other way round.

OLD NORSE SOURCES

The poem of *Solomon and Saturn* just referred to centres on a
riddle-contest, a form with two other prominent examples, both

in Old Norse. One is the *Vafðrúonismál*, one of twenty-nine poems in the *Elder* or *Poetic Edda*, a collection made in Iceland
perhaps about AD 1200. Tolkien knew this well, drawing on the
poem *Völuspá* for the names of the dwarves in *The Hobbit*, on
the *Fáfnismál* for the conversation with Smaug, and on the *Skir-
nismál* for the 'tribes of orcs' and the 'Misty Mountains'. More
generally the whole collection gives a sharper edge than *Beowulf* to the ideal of heroism, and a stronger sense of a tumul-
tuous history filtering down to echo and hearsay. Both points are
well brought out in the old, now-superseded edition of the *Cor-
pus Poeticum Boreale*, by Gudbrand Vigfusson and F. York Powell (1883), as also in Ursula Dronke's much later edition of four
poems, *The Poetic Edda, Volume I: Heroic Poems* (1969). There
is an old-fashioned translation of the whole of *The Poetic Edda*
by Lee M. Hollander (1962); a much better one has recently appeared, *Norse Poems*, by Paul B. Taylor and W.H. Auden (1981).
An earlier version of this last was dedicated to Tolkien.

The other major riddle-contest in Old Norse appears in *The
Saga of King Heidrek the Wise*, edited and translated by Christopher Tolkien (1960). The relevance of this to all Tolkien's work,
including *The Silmarillion*, should be obvious; the combination
of pride, ferocity and sadness in the older poem of 'The Battle of
the Goths and Huns' which has found its way into the saga
seems to be the note that Tolkien often aimed at, and as often
disapproved. Another *fornaldarsaga* or 'saga of old times' of
much interest to Tolkien readers is the *Völsunga Saga*; William
Morris's translation of it in 1870 was reprinted with an introduction by Robert W. Putnam (1962) and it has also been edited
and translated by R.G. Finch in the same series as Christopher
Tolkien's *Heidrek* (1965). Meanwhile the other great work of Old
Norse mythology, later and more 'novelistic' in tone than the poems, is the *Prose Edda* of Snorri Sturluson, written in Iceland between 1225 and 1241. This too is a work of 'mediation', like
Tolkien's; Snorri was a Christian trying to preserve pagan material for his countrymen and for the cause of poetry. In several
ways, especially its combination of respect for antiquity with a
certain detached humour, Snorri prefigures Tolkien. One of the
'lost' poems known only by its quotations was a model for 'Al-
darion and Erendis'; . . . another poem added to a manuscript of
Snorri's *Edda* by some well-wisher is the *Rígsthula*. . . . There is
a good translation of most of Snorri's work in *The Prose Edda*,
trans. Jean I. Young (1966).

Nineteenth-Century Fairy-Tale Collections

It is a jump of many centuries to the great 'fairy-tale' collections of the nineteenth, but . . . Jacob Grimm at least thought the similarity between German fairy-tale and Scandinavian 'Edda' striking enough to prove that both were the debris of a greater unity. Whether this is so or not, the folk-tales of North-West Europe affected Tolkien profoundly. The three major collections (from his point of view) were probably those by the brothers Grimm, printed first in 1812, but expanded, revised and translated ever since: I have used *The Complete Grimm's Fairy Tales*, no translator named, published in London by Routledge and Kegan Paul in 1975, but Tolkien certainly read them in German––he relished the dialect forms of 'Von dem Machandelboom', quoting it in the original in 'On Fairy-Stories' (*TL*, p. 32). Another work he refers to is *Popular Tales from the Norse*, collected by P.C. Asbjörnsen and J.I. Moe and translated by Sir George Dasent, published first in English in Edinburgh, 1859, but reprinted in London by The Bodley Head, 1969. In the same modern series (1968) is *English Fairy Tales* by Joseph Jacobs, a reprint from 1890; No. 21, 'Childe Rowland' is a 'Dark Tower' story. . . . Tolkien also quoted from J.F. Campbell's *Popular Tales of the Western Highlands* (1890–3).

Ballads

Parallel to the fairy-tale tradition collected by the Grimms and others is the ballad tradition, also preserved by collectors of the nineteenth century and containing much similar, and similarly archaic material. The greatest collection of these is certainly F.J. Child's *The English and Scottish Popular Ballads*, first published in five volumes by Houghton Mifflin, Boston, 1882–98, and reprinted by Dover Publications, New York, 1965. Particularly vital to this are the philological introductions to each ballad, see especially no. 19, 'King Orfeo', no. 60, 'King Estmere', and others; while Tolkien also almost certainly read Lowry C. Wimberly's commentary *Folklore in the English and Scottish Ballads* (1928). Tolkien probably also knew the Danish collection begun by Svend Grundtvig, *Danmarks gamle Folkeviser*, out in 12 volumes from 1853 onwards, and partly available to English readers in *A Book of Danish Ballads*, ed. Axel Olrik, trans. E.M. Smith-Dampier (1939). The collection includes several elf-and-mortal or mermaid-and-mortal ballads like Tolkien's own poems. . . . The collector's father, Nicolai Grundtvig, was in my opinion the 'Beowulfian' whom Tolkien most respected—he appears, in 'Monsters' as one of the 'very old voices' calling ' "it is a mythical allegory" . . . generally shouted down, but not so far out as some of the newer cries'. Grundtvig senior was also remarkable for his efforts to reconcile his studies in pagan antiquity with his position as evangelistic reformer and 'apostle of the North', arguing for Óthinn as a 'forerunner', Earendel-like, of the Messiah, both 'sons of the Universal Father'.

AMERICAN TRADITIONS

But Tolkien was also interested in later traditions, and even in American traditions: anyone who reads the 'Introduction' to *English Folk-Songs from the Southern Appalachians* (1917) will be struck by the strange resemblance of the mountain country of North Carolina before the First World War to 'the Shire' as Tolkien described it. Nor is this accident. A piece by Mr Guy Davenport in the *New York Times* (23 February 1979) records Tolkien grilling an American classmate of his for 'tales of Kentucky folk . . . family names like Barefoot and Boffin and Baggins and good country names like that'. *Old* country names, one might add: in Kentucky and its neighbours, Tolkien obviously thought, there had for a time been a place where English people and English traditions could flourish by themselves free of the chronic imperialism of Latin, Celtic and French. In the same way Fenimore Cooper's hero Natty Bumppo prides himself on being 'a man whose blood is without a cross'; and Tolkien recorded an early devotion to Red Indians, bows and arrows and forests ('OFS' in *TL*, p. 39). The journey of the Fellowship from Lórien to Tol Brandir, with its canoes and portages, often recalls *The Last of the Mohicans*, and as the travellers move from forest to prairie, like the American pioneers, Aragorn and Éomer for a moment preserve faint traces of 'the Deerslayer' and the Sioux. . . . The complaint in one of the sillier reviews of *The Lord of the Rings*, that none of its characters (except Gimli) had 'an even faintly American temperament', is as imperceptive as irrelevant. . . .

MEDIEVAL INFLUENCES

The medieval or middle period between the high vernacular culture of North-West Europe and the collecting or 'reconstructing' era of Child and the Grimms was in several ways a disappointment to Tolkien, though of course he found much in its more traditional poems such as *Pearl, Sir Gawain* and *Sir Orfeo*. His translations of these must be recommended (see 'Abbreviations' under *SGPO*), as also the edition of *Sir Gawain* by himself and E.V. Gordon (*SGGK*), and of *Pearl* by E.V. Gordon alone (1953). Tolkien's assistance to the latter is acknowledged. Tolkien also lived for many years with the *Ancrene Riwle*, or *Ancrene Wisse*, and those concerned to seek out an influence on him might read *The Ancrene Riwle*, translated by Mary Salu, a pupil of his (1955). That work was written *c.* 1225, in Herefordshire. Close in both place and time was the *Brut*, an Arthurian Chronicle-epic by one Layamon. Tolkien certainly valued this as a repository of past tradition, borrowing from it, for instance, Éowyn's word 'dwimmerlaik'. At some stage he must also have noted that the stream by which the poet lived—it is a tributary of the Severn—was the River Gladdon. Part of the poem can be found in *Selections from Layamon's Brut*, ed. G.L. Brook with preface by C.S. Lewis (1963). I am also persuaded that Tolkien found stimulus in the slightly later legends of St Michael and St Brendan in *The Early South English Legendary*, edited by C. Horstmann for the Early English Text Society (1887).

Two other clear medieval English influences on Tolkien are *Mandeville's Travels*, written about 1375, and available in a modern translation by M.C. Seymour (1968); and the *Lais* of Marie de France, also available in translation by Eugene Mason (1911). The latter is a clear source for 'Aotrou and Itroun', the former perhaps the best guide to Tolkien's notions of the trees of Sun and Moon, the *Paradis terrestre*, and the road to it encumbered by enchantments like those of the Dead Marshes. Many phrases from this book seem to have stayed in Tolkien's mind. One should add that for all their names and preferred languages, both 'Sir John Mandeville' and Marie de France were certainly English by nationality.

Dealing with Tolkien's knowledge of other languages could protract this essay interminably, but a source of the highest importance was clearly the Finnish epic *Kalevala*, which Tolkien knew in the translation of W.F. Kirby (1907).... Also recommendable is the Irish *imram, The Voyage of Bran Son of Febal*, ed. Kuno, Meyer (1895-7). Tolkien's wanderings in German romance, though probably considerable, . . . are too complex for me to trace. Some guides through the wilderness of heroic legend can be found, however, in the philologists: and when it comes to it these were the men whom Tolkien probably followed with the keenest and most professional interest. Three major works may be cited, though they give the interested reader no more than a taste: *Grimm's Teutonic Mythology*, trans. J.S. Stallybrass (1882–8); R.W. Chambers, *Widsith, a Study in Old English Heroic Legend* (1912); and R.M. Wilson, *The Lost Literature of Medieval England* (1952). It should be noted that a vital part of this latter came out as early as 1941, in plenty of time for Tolkien to recall it in *The Lord of the Rings*. . . .

HISTORIES AND CHRONICLES

The last major 'old' source for Tolkien which need be mentioned lies in history and chronicle. Gibbon's *Decline and Fall of the Roman Empire* certainly stayed in Tolkien's mind, though probably in the same compartment as Wagner; 'Radagaisus' may be found in its 'Index', if not 'Radagast', as also 'Fredegarius', though not 'Frodo'. Of the Latin histories which Gibbon used the most interesting for Tolkien were probably Saxo Grammaticus's *History of the Danes*, of which Books 1–9 were translated by Oliver Elton, with an introduction by F. York Powell (1894); and *The Gothic History of Jordanes* translated by C.C. Mierow (1915). One has to add that Mr Mierow's grasp of Gothic, unlike his Latin, is feeble. The true opinions of Jordanes lie buried in Karl Müllenhoff's notes to Mommsen's edition of 1882. A final note on the Germanic tribes as they appealed to Tolkien's imagination may be found in Sir Charles Oman's classic, *A History of the Art of War in the Middle Ages* (1898). Its description on pp. 48–51 of the Lombards, that other Germanic 'horse-folk' *par excellence*, strongly recalls the Riders of the Mark.

MODERN WRITERS

When it comes to modern writers, Tolkien was notoriously beyond influence (though reports of his skimpy reading have been much exaggerated. . .). Three authors of his youth must remain prominent in any account. One is George MacDonald, whose influence Tolkien both admitted and minimised, see references in the 'Index' to *Letters:* besides *The Princess and the Goblin* of 1872 and *The Princess and Curdie* ten years later one should note especially *Phantastes* (1858) and *Lilith* (1895). Tolkien also read William Morris, probably with more appreciation: Morris after all knew a good deal of Icelandic and had been stirred by heroic story, trying to reproduce its effects in three of the romances of his last years, *The House of the Wolfings* (1888), *The Roots of the Mountains* (1889) and *The Glittering Plain* (1891). The first is clearly about Goths; the second gave a hint for Gollum, as for Brodda the Easterling in *The Silmarillion*; the last is about a quest for the Undying Lands. In my introduction to the World's Classics 1980 reprint of Morris's *The Wood at the World's End* (1894) I suggest a slight connection between that and the bewilderments of Fangorn Forest. Finally—though Tolkien never mentions him in a letter—I cannot help thinking that Tolkien knew Kipling's stories well, especially the collections *Puck of Pook's Hill* (1906) and *Rewards and Fairies* (1910). In both the theme of an unchanging Englishness is strong, as is that of smithcraft; and Puck's dislike for the word 'fairies' and the 'sugar-and-shake-your-head' Victorian concepts attached is exactly that of Tolkien (see especially the story 'Weland's Sword').

A RETURN TO ENGLISH TRADITIONS

I do not think Tolkien would have had much time for Kipling's 'Indian' works. The centre of all that has been mentioned in this essay is English tradition, though Tolkien was prepared to accept connections by blood with Iceland or Saxony or America, and (in a more gingerly way) by old proximity with the Irish or even the Finns. However he was in some ways what would now be called an 'ethnic' writer, though the rule for 'ethnicity' seems to be that anyone can have it *except Anglo-Saxons* (Tolkien was not quite a WASP). Largely this restriction is a penalty of success; since English is international the language naturally ceases to carry strong national sentiment. Behind that success, though, Tolkien was conscious of many centuries of discouragement which had suppressed native tradition in England more quickly, perhaps, than in any other European country. He valued what was left the more highly. In much of what he wrote and read one can see him trying to return to the time before confusion set in, when the traditions of the Shire and the Mark were uncorrupted.

ABBREVIATIONS

Letters   *Letters of J.R.R. Tolkien*, edited by Humphrey Carpenter with the assistance of Christopher Tolkien (London: George Allen & Unwin, 1981).

'OFS'   'On Fairy-Stories', see *TL* below.

'Preface'   Preface to *Beowulf and the Finnesburg Fragment: a Translation into Modern English* by J.R. Clark Hall, revised by C.L. Wrenn (London: George Allen & Unwin, 1940).

SGGK   *Sir Gawain and the Green Knight,* edited by J.R.R. Tokien and E.V. Gordon (Oxford: Clarendon Press, 1925).

SGPO   *Sir Gawain and the Green Knight, Pearl and Sir Orfeo,* translated by J.R.R. Tolkien, edited and with a preface by Christopher Tolkien (London: George Allen & Unwin, 1975).

TL   *Tree and Leaf* (London: George Allen & Unwin, 1964). This contains both 'Leaf by Niggle' and 'On Fairy-Stories', first published in 1945 and 1947 respectively. References to both are by page in this volume.

CHRONOLOGY

1892

John Ronald Reuel Tolkien, called Ronald, is born January 3, in Bloemfontein, the capital of Orange Free State, South Africa.

1894

Hilary Tolkien is born February 17.

1895

Mabel Suffield Tolkien, Ronald's mother, returns to England with her sons to visit her family.

1896

Arthur Reuel Tolkien, Ronald's father, dies in South Africa on February 15.

1899

The Boers (Dutch settlers; the word is Dutch for "farmer") of South Africa declare war on the British.

1900

Mabel Tolkien, along with her sons, converts to Roman Catholicism. Ronald enters King Edward VI School. Britain annexes the Boer Republic of South Africa, renaming it the Transvaal Colony; a guerrilla war will drag on for two years.

1902

The Boers of South Africa surrender unconditionally to the British, bringing the Boer War to an end; the Boers are made citizens of the British Empire.

1903

A scholarship student at King Edward VI School, Tolkien studies Middle English and Greek.

1904

Mabel Tolkien dies in England from complications of diabetes. Father Francis Morgan, their parish priest, becomes guardian of Ronald and Hilary.

1905

Ronald and his brother move in with their Aunt Beatrice.

1908

Unhappy at their aunt's, Ronald and Hilary move to Mrs. Faulkner's boardinghouse; Ronald meets Edith Bratt.

1910

Tolkien publishes several editorials, reports, articles (including at least one in Latin), and a poem in the King Edward VI School *Chronicle* from November 1910 through July 1911. He becomes a debater—in Anglo-Saxon, Greek, and Gothic—while also studying Old Norse and Spanish.

1911

With friends Christopher Wiseman, R.Q. Wilson, and later Geoffrey B. Smith, Tolkien creates the "T.C.B.S." (Tea Club and Barrovian Society). He enters Exeter College at Oxford University on a scholarship to study classics, but eventually specializes in comparative philology.

1915

After he takes a First Class degree in English from Oxford (specializing in Old and Middle English), he enters the British army. Commissioned a second lieutenant in the Lancashire Fusiliers, he begins training.

1916

Tolkien marries Edith Bratt. After serving in the Battle of the Somme (as batallion signalling officer), he is invalided out of the fray in November with an intractable case of trench fever (a disease carried by lice, characterized by a high fever). His friends R.Q. Wilson and Geoffrey Smith die in the war.

1917

While convalescing (he spends much of this year in the hospital), Tolkien begins to write *The Book of Lost Tales*, which will eventually become *The Silmarillion*. His first son, John, is born.

1918

Now a full lieutenant, Tolkien receives postings within England. After the armistice in November, he returns to Oxford and begins work as a junior staff member on the *Oxford New English Dictionary*.

1920

Tolkien is appointed reader in English language (a teaching position) at Leeds University. His second son, Michael, is born.

1922

Publishes *A Middle English Vocabulary.* Two Britons, Howard Carter and Lord Carnarvon, discover the relatively untouched tomb of Tutankhamen in Egypt's Valley of the Kings. James Joyce's *Ulysses* is published in France. T.S. Eliot publishes *The Waste Land;* Herman Hesse publishes *Siddhartha.*

1924

Tolkien is made professor of English language at Leeds (the youngest person to have held this position). His third son, Christopher, is born.

1925

Publishes *Sir Gawain and the Green Knight,* which he co-edited with E.V. Gordon. Moves from Leeds to Oxford when he is named Rawlinson and Bosworth Professor of Anglo-Saxon at Oxford University.

1926

Becomes friends with C.S. Lewis, who joins the Oxford faculty. Lewis and other friends (all Oxford dons) join an informal reading club, the Coalbiters, formed by Tolkien. A.A. Milne publishes *Winnie the Pooh.*

1929

His daughter, Priscilla, is born.

1930

Begins writing *The Hobbit.*

1931

The Inklings literary society is founded by an Oxford undergraduate, Tangye Lean, for the purpose of reading unpublished works; Tolkien and Lewis are among those who attend and read their works in progress. The British government's severe economic measures cause rioting in the streets of London and Glasgow. Great Britain abandons the gold standard, which erodes confidence in the banking system.

1932

The Protective Tariffs Acts end free trade, helping restore economic stability in Great Britain. Aldous Huxley publishes *Brave New World.*

1933

As Adolf Hitler gains power in Germany, the Oxford Union, the university's debating society, debates this proposition:

"That this House will in no circumstances fight for its King and Country." The pacifist position wins 275 to 153.

1936

Tolkien delivers his lecture "*Beowulf:* The Monsters and the Critics," to the British Academy. Included in *Proceedings of the British Academy* for 1936, it will also be published separately the following year.

1937

Publishes *The Hobbit, or There and Back Again.* At the suggestion of his publisher, Allen and Unwin, Tolkien begins work on a sequel, which will become *The Lord of the Rings.* Neville Chamberlain becomes prime minister, announcing as his goal the achievement of peace in Europe, which he will pursue by offering concessions to Germany and Italy.

1938

The *New York Herald Tribune* awards the American edition of *The Hobbit* its prize as best juvenile book of the year.

1939

Tolkien delivers the 1939 Andrew Lang Lecture, "On Fairy Stories." Germany begins annexing smaller European countries; in August it signs a nonaggression pact with Russia, and on September 1 invades Poland. On September 3, Great Britain and France declare war on Germany; World War II has begun. The United States declares neutrality, but will enter the war in 1941.

1940

Germany launches the Battle of Britain in August, intended to destroy the Royal Air Force in preparation for the invasion of England. Germany defeats France, invades Norway, and overruns Denmark, Luxembourg, Belgium, and the Netherlands. Winston Churchill becomes prime minister.

1945

Tolkien is named Merton Professor of English Language and Literature at Oxford University. Germany surrenders May 7. The United States drops the world's first atomic bombs on the Japanese cities of Hiroshima (August 6) and Nagasaki (August 9); Japan surrenders August 14.

1947

"On Fairy-Stories" is published in *Essays Presented to Charles Williams,* along with contributions from Dorothy L. Sayers, C.S. Lewis, A.O. Barfield, Gervase Mathew, and W. H. Lewis.

1949

Tolkien publishes *Farmer Giles of Ham.*

1950

Tolkien offers *The Lord of the Rings* to Collins publishers. They will decline to publish it and return it in 1952.

1951

Publishes a revised edition of *The Hobbit, or There and Back Again.*

1954

Publishes *The Fellowship of the Ring: Being the First Part of The Lord of the Rings* and *The Two Towers: Being the Second Part of The Lord of the Rings.*

1955

Publishes *The Return of the King: Being the Third Part of The Lord of the Rings.*

1959

Retires from Oxford University.

1962

Publishes *Ancrene Wisse: The English Text of the Ancrene Riwle* and *The Adventures of Tom Bombadil and Other Verses from The Red Book.*

1964

Publishes *Tree and Leaf.*

1965

Ace Books publishes an unauthorized American edition of *The Lord of the Rings,* without offering royalties to the author. After Tolkien spreads the word about the unauthorized edition and readers reject the Ace edition in favor of the more expensive authorized version, Ace agrees to pay royalties on all the books it has sold. Meanwhile, helped by Ace's promotion of the book, a "campus cult" has formed around the books. American enthusiasm for Tolkien spreads to other countries, and "suddenly," several years after original publication, the books become tremendous best-sellers (selling around 3 million copies around the world by the end of 1968).

1966

Publishes third edition of *The Hobbit, or There and Back Again* (he will continue to make corrections in subsequent editions).

1967

Publishes *Smith of Wootton Major.*

1968

Ronald and Edith Tolkien move to Lakeside, Pool (near Bournemouth, England).

1971

Edith Tolkien dies.

1972

Tolkien returns to Oxford to live. He is awarded the C.B.E. (Commander of the Order of the British Empire), and Oxford University confers on him an honorary doctorate of letters.

1973

While visiting friends in Bournemouth, Tolkien falls ill. He dies September 2.

1975

Tolkien's translation of *Sir Gawain and the Green Knight, Pearl, and Sir Orfeo,* edited by Christopher Tolkien, is published.

1976

The Father Christmas Letters is published, edited by Baillie Tolkien (Christopher's wife). (This edition contains more of the letters and text than are found in subsequent editions.)

1977

The Silmarillion, edited by Christopher Tolkien, is published.

1979

Pictures by J.R.R. Tolkien, with foreword and notes by Christopher Tolkien, is published; a revised edition will be published in 1992.

1981

Letters of J.R.R. Tolkien: A Selection, edited by Humphrey Carpenter, with the assistance of Christopher Tolkien, is published. *The Old English Exodus,* with text, translation, and commentary by J.R.R. Tolkien, edited by Joan Turville-Petre, is published.

1983–1996

Twelve volumes in *The History of Middle-earth* series (edited by Christopher Tolkien) are published. They are greatly anticipated by fans still fascinated by Tolkien's original saga.

1998

Roverandom, a children's book by Tolkien, edited by Christina Scull and Wayne G. Hammond, is published.

FOR FURTHER RESEARCH

Alida Becker, ed., *The Tolkien Scrapbook.* New York: Grosset & Dunlap, 1978.

Humphrey Carpenter, *The Inklings.* Boston: Houghton Mifflin, 1979.

———, *Tolkien: A Biography.* Boston: Houghton Mifflin, 1977.

Lin Carter, *Tolkien: A Look Behind* The Lord of the Rings. New York: Ballantine, 1969.

Jane Chance, *The Lord of the Rings: The Mythology of Power.* New York: Twayne, 1992.

Katharyn F. Crabbe, *J.R.R. Tolkien.* New York: Frederick Ungar, 1981.

Robley Evans, *J.R.R. Tolkien.* Writers for the 70s series. New York: Crowell, 1972.

Verlyn Flieger, *A Question of Time: J.R.R. Tolkien's Road to Faerie.* Kent, OH: Kent State University Press, 1997.

Robert Foster, *A Guide to Middle-earth.* New York: Ballantine, 1971. (New edition published 1978. See also the entry for the 1990 edition below, under "Interesting and Helpful Editions.")

Robert Giddings, ed., *J.R.R. Tolkien: This Far Land.* Totowa, NJ: Barnes & Noble, 1984.

David Harvey, *The Song of Middle-earth: J.R.R. Tolkien's Themes, Symbols and Myths.* London: Allen & Unwin, 1985.

Randel Helms, *Tolkien's World.* Boston: Houghton Mifflin, 1974.

Mark Robert Hillegas, ed., *Shadows of Imagination: The Fantasies of C.S. Lewis, J.R.R. Tolkien, and Charles Williams.* Crosscurrents/Modern Techniques series. With an afterword on J.R.R. Tolkien's *The Silmarillion* by Peter Kreeft. Carbondale: Southern Illinois University Press, 1979.

Neil D. Isaacs and Rose A. Zimbardo, eds., *Tolkien and the*

Critics. Notre Dame, IN: University of Notre Dame Press, 1968.

———, *Tolkien: New Critical Perspectives*. Lexington: University Press of Kentucky, 1981.

Clyde S. Kilby, *Tolkien and the Silmarillion*. Wheaton, IL: Harold Shaw, 1976.

Paul H. Kocher, *Master of Middle-earth: The Fiction of J.R.R. Tolkien*. Boston: Houghton Mifflin, 1972.

Jared Lobdell, ed., *A Tolkien Compass: Including J.R.R. Tolkien's Guide to the Names in* The Lord of the Rings. LaSalle, IL: Open Court, 1975.

Richard Mathews, *Lightning from a Clear Sky: Tolkien, the Trilogy, and the Silmarillion*. Milford Popular Writers of Today series. San Bernardino, CA: Borgo Press, 1978.

Stephen O. Miller, *Middle Earth: A World in Conflict*. Baltimore: T-K Graphics, 1975.

Charles W.R.D. Moseley, *J.R.R. Tolkien*. Writers and Their Work series. Plymouth, UK: Northcote House, in association with the British Council, 1997.

Jane Chance Nitzsche, *Tolkien's Art: A "Mythology for England."* New York: St. Martin's Press, 1979.

Ruth S. Noel, *The Languages of Middle-earth*. Boston: Houghton Mifflin, 1980.

———, *The Mythology of Middle-earth*. Boston: Houghton Mifflin, 1977.

Timothy R. O'Neill, *The Individuated Hobbit: Jung, Tolkien, and the Archetypes of Middle-earth*. Boston: Houghton Mifflin, 1979.

Anne C. Petty, *One Ring to Bind Them All: Tolkien's Mythology*. University: University of Alabama Press, 1979.

Richard L. Purtill, *J.R.R. Tolkien: Myth, Morality, and Religion*. San Francisco: Harper & Row, 1984.

———, *Lord of the Elves and Eldils: Fantasy and Philosophy in C.S. Lewis and J.R.R. Tolkien*. Grand Rapids, MI: Zondervan, 1974.

Roger Sale, *Modern Heroism: Essays on D.H. Lawrence, William Empson, and J.R.R. Tolkien*. Berkeley and Los Angeles: University of California Press, 1973.

Mary Salu and Robert T. Farrell, eds., *J.R.R. Tolkien, Scholar and Storyteller: Essays in Memoriam*. Ithaca, NY: Cornell University Press, 1979.

T.A. Shippey, *The Road to Middle-earth.* Boston: Houghton Mifflin, 1983.

J.E.A. Tyler, *The New Tolkien Companion.* New York: St. Martin's Press, 1979. Supersedes Tyler's *The Tolkien Companion* of 1976 by the same publisher.

Richard C. West, *Tolkien Criticism: An Annotated Checklist.* Kent, OH: Kent State University Press, 1970. Revised edition, 1981.

INTERESTING AND HELPFUL EDITIONS

J.R.R. Tolkien, *The Annotated Hobbit.* Introduction and notes by Douglas A. Anderson. Boston: Houghton Mifflin, 1988.

———, *The Peoples of Middle-earth.* Ed. Christopher Tolkien. London: HarperCollins, 1996. (*The History of Middle-earth* 12) This final volume in the series includes a history of the Appendices to *The Lord of the Rings.*

———, "Guide to the names in *The Lord of the Rings,*" in *A Tolkien Compass,* ed. Jared Lobdell. LaSalle, IL: Open Court, 1975.

J.R.R. Tolkien and Robert Foster, *The Complete Guide to Middle-earth: From* The Hobbit *to* The Silmarillion. 1971. Reprint, New York: Ballantine, July 1990.

Revised editions of *The Lord of the Rings* trilogy were published by Ballantine (New York) in 1965. A further revised edition was published by Allen and Unwin (London) in 1966, and further corrections were made in later British editions. Houghton Mifflin's 1987 edition (Boston) attempted to include all the changes from the British editions as well as some corrections that appeared only in the Ballantine edition. HarperCollins (London) published the Houghton Mifflin version with further corrections in 1994.

TOLKIEN ON THE INTERNET

Many websites focus on various aspects of Tolkien and his work, including such specialized interests as linguistics, Tolkien's art and maps, character histories and genealogies, and biographical material. A good place to start is the Tolkien Network, with links to many Tolkien sites: www.tolkien.nu. Some sites feature audio downloads, which allow you to hear the author's voice; one such site offers both a ten-minute BBC interview with the author from 1971 and a written transcript of the interview: http://village.vossnet.co.uk/h/hpttrsn/jrrt_int.htm.

INDEX